The Major Prophets

by Jack P. Lewis

The Major Prophets

The Major Prophets

*Lessons to study
and teach
from the Old Testament
Books of Isaiah, Jeremiah,
Ezekiel, and Daniel*

Jack P. Lewis
Memphis, Tennessee

Hester Publications, 165 Gibson Drive, Henderson, Tennessee 38340
Printed in the United States of America
Publisher: Samuel E. Hester
Cover design: J. Algene Steele
First Printing: September 1999

TABLE OF CONTENTS

The Major Prophets

LIST OF ABBREVIATIONS

Adv. Haer. Adversus Haeresies.

Adv. Jov. Adversus Jovinianum.

ANET^3. Ancient Near Eastern Texts Relating to the Old Testament, James B. Pritchard, editor, third edition.

Ant. Antiquities of the Jews.

Apol. Apology.

b. Babylonian Talmud.

BASOR Bulletin of American Schools of Oriental Research.

BDB F. Brown, S.R. Driver, and C. Briggs, *A Hebrew and English Lexicon of the Old Testament* (Oxford: Clarendon Press, 1952).

KBS L. Koehler, W. Baumgartner, and J.J. Stamm, *The Hebrew and Aramaic Lexicon of the Old Testament* (Leiden: Brill, 1994).

Men. *Menahoth.*

N.T. New Testament.

O.T. Old Testament.

P.L. Migne, *Patrologia series latina.*

Bible Versions

ASV American Standard Version.

KJV King James Version.

LXX Septuagint.

NIV New International Version.

NRSV New Revised Standard Version.

RSV Revised Standard Version.

TEV Today's English Version.

The Major Prophets

Chapter I

AN INTRODUCTION

Major Prophets

The five books (Isaiah, Jeremiah, Lamentations, Ezekiel, and Daniel), known to students of the English Bible as the Major Prophets, do not really form a unified body of material. They are not from the same historical period; the literary forms in which they are written are not identical; nor is the history of their preservation and transmission unified.

The oldest division of the Hebrew books is not the fivefold division familiar to English Bible students but is threefold with three categories: Law, Prophets and Writings. In this division the Prophets are subdivided into Former Prophets (Joshua, Judges, Samuel, and Kings) and Latter Prophets (Isaiah, Jeremiah, Ezekiel, and the Twelve Prophets). Lamentations and Daniel in this classification fall in the third division—The Writings. However, the Greek Bible (the Septuagint) arranged books in a different sequence from that followed in the Hebrew Bible. The Latin Bible followed the Greek, and in turn Latin determined the English Bible classification.

We owe the designation "Major Prophets" to Augustine's characterization of the twelve prophets as "Minor Prophets":

> The prophecy of Isaiah is not in the book of
> the twelve prophets who are called minor from
> the brevity of their writings, as compared with
> those who are called the greater prophets because
> they published larger volumes (*City of God,*
> 18:29).

The designation "major" has no implication of the importance of these prophets. Who is to say that Amos is of less significance than Isaiah that one should be minor and the other major? The time of the writing of the books also is not under consideration in the terminology. Amos came about 750 B.C. at the beginning of Israel's prophetic literary movement while Ezekiel came two centuries later in the exilic period. The length of the books makes some prophets "major" and others "minor" though even this distinction is not altogether valid since Lamentations is shorter than are some of the "minor prophets." Lamentations is not a prophetic book at all. Its location in the classification is due to its traditional connection with the prophet Jeremiah. The traditional English heading (dropped in *Today's English Version, New International Version, New Revised Standard Version, Revised English Bible, New Living Translation, and Contemporary English Version*) is "Lamentations of Jeremiah." The Hebrew title is merely *'echah* ("How") taken from the book's opening words of chapters 1, 2, and 4.

The Prophet

The prophet was the man through whose organs of speech God spoke to his people. God placed his message in the prophet's mouth (Exod. 4:15f.; 7:1; Jer. 15:19), and the prophet spoke to the people. "Thus says the Lord" (Ezek. 6:11; Amos 1:3), "the spirit of the Lord is upon me" (Isa. 61:1; cf. 1 Chron. 12:18), "the word of the Lord came to me" (Ezek. 3:16), "the hand of the Lord was upon me" (Ezek. 3:14), and "says the Lord" (Amos 4;6; etc) are some of the common ways of expressing the prophetic impulse.

The Hebrew word *nabhi'*, the most common word for the prophet, is now thought to designate one who has been called to his task. The prophet is also called "a seer" (*ro'eh* [1 Sam. 9:9] and *chozeh* [2 Chron. 33:18]), "a man of the spirit" (Hos. 9:7), "a man of God" (1 Sam. 9:6; 1 Kings 13:1), and derogatorily spoken of as being crazy (2 Kings 9:11; Jer. 29:26; Hos. 9:7). Amos, Isaiah, Jeremiah, and Ezekiel all narrate experiences that might be designated their "call" to service. A variety of men from the shepherd, the priest, to the courtier were called and equipped for their tasks.

Though Abraham (Gen. 20:7) and Moses (Deut. 18:15; 34:10-11) are called prophets, it is Samuel who begins a new period in prophetic activity. At his time there appeared groups of prophets, in Elijah's and Elisha's time groups are called "sons of the prophets," and from this time many distinctive personalities are seen. About the early prophets the Bible relates episodes in which the prophets were active but preserves very little of their actual oracles. In this group we encounter men like Samuel, Nathan, Elijah, Elisha, and Micaiah ben Imlah. Their activities center in the northern kingdom. The book of Kings gives more space to the northern kingdom until its demise than to the southern kingdom.

The book of Chronicles which centers on the kings of Judah makes clear that prophets were also active there. The man of God, Shemaiah, instructed Rehoboam not to attempt to regain control over the revolting tribes by force (1 Kings 12:22-24). Iddo is said to have written of Judean kings (2 Chron. 13:22). Azariah, son of Oded, spoke to Asa (2 Chron. 15:1-7) as did Hanani the seer (2 Chron. 16:7-10). Jehu, son of Hanani, and Jahaziel spoke to Jehoshaphat (2 Chron. 19:2-3; 20:14-17). Jehu is said to have written a Chronicle (2 Chron. 20:34). There were unnamed prophets during the reign of Joash (2 Chron. 24:19), and Zechariah son of Jehoiada was killed at Joash's command (2 Chron. 24:20-22). An unnamed man of God advised Amaziah against hiring soldiers from Israel (2 Chron. 25:7-10).

Around the middle of the eighth century B.C., however, a change came in prophecy in that oracles of the prophets were collected together and preserved in the form of books. Amos and Hosea are active in the northern kingdom, but most of the writing prophets deal with Judah. Relatively few personal episodes are related about these writing prophets. Biographies could not be written of any of them, but we know from their books a great deal about what they had to say.

The details of the making of a prophetic book are a matter of great dispute in current scholarship. In particular, the part played by the prophet's disciples in the preservation of the prophet's oracles is debated. We have very little information, and most of that which is said is speculation. The teacher-disciple relationship is seen in Elijah and Elisha, but not often elsewhere. Isaiah ordered, "Bind up the testimony, seal the teaching among my disciples" (Isa. 8:16). He is commanded by the Lord to write down what he had to say "that it may be for the time to come as a witness forever (Isa. 30:8).

Jeremiah was instructed to write all the words the Lord had spoken to him (Jer. 30:2). The nearest description of the writing of a prophetic book is the narration of Jeremiah's experience in dictating his oracles to Baruch. Jehoiakim burned that copy, and Jeremiah at the instruction of the Lord dictated the oracles for a second time and added much more (Jer. 36). However, the second copy could not be our present book of Jeremiah since canonical Jeremiah has many oracles dated later than the fourth year of Jehoiakim to which this episode is assigned.

A valid case can be made for the appearance of Israel's prophets when dangers confronted the nation. Samuel appeared when the Philistines were threatening. It is also at this time that Israel's monarchy appeared. Elijah opposed Jezebel's efforts to foster the worship of Baal in Israel. Elisha was active during the Aramean wars. Israel's confrontation with Assyria occasioned the prophecies of Amos, Hosea, Micah, Isaiah, Zephaniah, and Nahum. A century later than Amos and Isaiah, the clash with Babylon gave rise to the prophecies of Habakkuk and Jeremiah. Ezekiel and Daniel come to the fore during the Babylonian exile and its problems. There are also prophets of the post-exilic period like Haggai, Zechariah, and Malachi who dealt with problems of that time.

Except for some portions of Isaiah, each of the Major Prophets deals with history after Israel (the Northern Kingdom) had gone into exile in 722 B.C. and was no more. They draw lessons from Israel's history and fate, but their concerns are primarily with Judah and its fortunes. The student interested in backgrounds should study biblical history beginning at 2 Kings 15:27ff. and 2 Chronicles 26:1ff. to see the vicissitudes of the period of the Major Prophets.

Isaiah

Isaiah prophesied in Jerusalem under the kings Uzziah, Jotham, Ahaz, and Hezekiah and exercised an influence on the policies of these kings. International policies of the time are a major concern of his. His contemporary Micah, whose book is classified in the Minor Prophets, was concerned primarily with social conditions of his own area, with the Assyrian invasion, and with its impact upon the foothill region about Moresheth-gath from where he came. Micah does not appear as the advisor of kings.

In Isaiah's day the political policies followed by Hezekiah were building up to a major confrontation between the might of Assyria and the small Judean state which hoped to enlist the aid of Egypt so that she could throw off the Assyrian yoke which King Ahaz had earlier accepted. Not only does Isaiah deal with the ordinary sins of his people for which the Lord must punish them with his rod—Assyria, but he repeatedly warns of the futility of the political policy being followed. The Lord is Israel's safety, not Egypt. In 701 B.C. the confrontation with Assyria became a reality. Hezekiah revolted. Sennacherib came west, took forty-six of Hezekiah's walled cities and many unwalled villages, and shut him up in Jerusalem "like a bird in a cage." Only the intervention of God destroyed the Assyrian army at the last moment and saved the city.

The second part of Isaiah's book (chs. 40-66) deals with an entirely different time and with different matters. It envisions that the Babylonian exile has run its course. God's punishment of Judah has been sufficient. Cyrus, king of Persia, is being raised up as the Lord's agent to restore his people to their land. The Lord, the only God in existence, will accomplish his purpose. Kings are powerless in any opposition they might offer. Idols are helpless, and their worship is futile.

Jeremiah

Approximately one hundred years of Judean history rolled by after the time of Isaiah and the period assumed in the first section of the book of Isaiah before Jeremiah appeared on the scene. Meanwhile, Assyria had reached its zenith of power and had hastened toward its demise before the rising power of Babylon. Nineveh, attacked by the Medes, Scythians, and Babylonians, fell in 612 B.C.; and the battle of Carchemish in 605 B.C. brought a confrontation between the remnants of Assyria (which had fled westward to Haran) and Babylon. Assyria was aided by Neco of Egypt, but Nebuchadnezzar, crown prince of Babylon, came off victorious. Assyria and Egypt would never again be serious contenders for world domination.

Judah at this period passed under the rule of Babylon. In the face of these developments, Jeremiah arose as the prophet in Jerusalem. Across the reigns of Josiah, Jehoahaz, Jehoiakim, Jehoiachin, and Zedekiah, he stood as one man against the trends of the nation. Speaking out of intense inner conflict, he announced the approaching doom of the nation under blows from Nebuchadnezzar in 606, 597, and 586 B.C.

Jerusalem lost what independence she had retained. The prophet repeatedly spoke of the futility of the policies being followed. After the final fiasco, with Jerusalem in ruins and with Gedaliah the Babylonian appointed governor murdered, Jeremiah was carried against his will by his countrymen to Egypt where in vain he continued denouncing their idolatrous practices. We do not know his final fate.

Lamentations

The Book of Lamentations is of an entirely different literary category from that of the other Major Prophets. While the other books are ordinarily collections of the oracles of the prophet, Lamentations is a series of artistically constructed elegiac poems lamenting in a most graphic way the calamity which befell Jerusalem in 586 B.C. Out of a deep realization of the consequences of sin come to fruition, an eye-witness of the calamity pleads for the mercy of God on his city and upon his people. Claiming no merit on their part, the writer can only say, "God be merciful to us who are sinners."

Ezekiel

Ezekiel, in many ways the strangest of the prophets, is unique in that he received his call to prophesy outside of Palestine. Being a priest carried off with others of the upper classes in 597 B.C., his ministry is to the exiles in Babylon. Beginning in 592 B.C., he continued his work until after the fall of Jerusalem in 586 B.C. While Jeremiah in Jerusalem was announcing the coming calamity to the city, saying that the Exile was to last seventy years and advising those already in exile to settle down, build houses, and make a life for themselves in exile where they were, Ezekiel among the exiles was working to overcome a false optimism which supposed the exile would be over in two years. By symbolic act, by narrated vision, and by allegory he announced that Jerusalem must fall.

However, like his contemporary in Jerusalem, once his predictions had come to tragic reality, Ezekiel then set himself to overcome his people's despondency which set in and which threatened death to their faith. He spoke of the day which must arise out of the calamity. The Exile would eventually end and Judah would be restored to her own land. A great deal of Ezekiel's book likely was never delivered orally.

It is a literary production.

Daniel

The final one of our prophets, Daniel, has left us a book very different from any of the other four. The first portion of the book is composed of a series of six narratives about experiences of the prophet and his associates in the land of exile. These chapters contain little of the ordinary prophetic type oracle. Daniel and his companions were taken to Babylon in 606 B.C., but the narratives carry him on down into the reign of Darius of Persia which must be as late as 520 B.C. The second part of the book contains a series of visions seen by the prophet. These narrations fall into the literary category known as apocalyptic. In fact, they set the major literary conventions used by the succeeding writers of Jewish apocalypses. In them, the seer is taken on a trip through the heavens where he is shown things to be. History is related in animal symbolism. The vision is ordered sealed up because it belongs to the last times.

From this survey we see that the Major Prophets span the Assyrian, Babylonian, and Persian periods of Old Testament history. Isaiah prophesied at least as early at 735 B.C. Daniel is said to be active at least as late as the times of Darius, that is, down to 520 B.C. or later. We are, therefore, concerned with at least two centuries of Judean history in studying the Major Prophets. We have also seen that in literary form we have in this group of books the prophetic oracle, the narrative about the prophet, the poetic lament, and the beginning of apocalyptic. It is far from a unified body of material.

An Approach to the Prophets

In approaching the prophets there are three widespread misconceptions which need to be laid to rest. The first is the picture of the prophet which makes him primarily deal with esoteric mysteries concerning the coming of Christ. Early Christians searched the prophets for proof texts valuable in their controversies with the Jews. The effort was the more tempting because the New Testament explained numerous prophetic passages in a messianic way.

The rise of scientific exegesis has caused the proof texting exegesis to lose its appeal. The excesses of the church fathers are apparent to all who read them. While each of the Major Prophets (excluding Lamentations) has a legitimate messianic element, it is only a minor part of their content. Their social, moral, and religious teaching occupy far more space. Though we have not lost interest in the messianic element, we are actually stressing a different element in the prophets from that stressed by early Christians when we in these studies stress their social, moral, and religious values.

The second misconception approaches the prophets supposing that the high points of history of all times are to be found in them. They are made the predictors of airplanes, atomic bombs, and world wars both of current history and of history at the end time. This type of approach can be seen repeatedly in the sermon topics announced in the religious section of the local newspaper, in sermons delivered on television, or in the books of the Hal Lindsey type. One is supposed to be able to deduce from the prophets what the outcome of the Middle East crisis is to be and what Russia will do. But actually, the prophets primarily spoke to problems of their own day. Their enemy out of the north is not Russia which did not even exist in their day. Only after we determine what the prophets meant to their own day are we ready to ask what they can mean to us. We have no occasion to deny some predictive prophecy. The sign of the true prophet was the fulfillment of his oracles (Deut. 18:21-22; 1 Sam. 3:19-21), and the O.T. cites many cases of the fulfillment of prophecy, but the prophets were not primarily clairvoyants.

Yet a third misconception has made the prophets primarily to be social reformers and has tended to play down or to deny the predictive element in their oracles. Each writing prophet has some prediction in his oracles. This element cannot be denied, and to minimize it is to distort the prophets. The "foreteller" versus the "forthteller" antithesis of a prior generation is a false antithesis.

The study of the prophets, then, needs a balance in emphasis between the religious, social, and moral elements, and the predictive element in their message.

A sizable portion of the prophetic oracles is in rhythmical form. Recent English translations attempt to reproduce that rhythm in English poetry thereby making the prophets to be more readable and intelligible than they are when printed all in prose. These more recent translations also make use of vocabulary insights and light on poetic form which have been cast by archaeological study. They use English words in their current meanings, not in archaic ones. One will be benefited by studying the prophets in current translations.

Only by first determining what the prophets meant to the people of their own day can it successfully be determined what they must mean for us today. From studying their situation and what they had to say to it one can come to see that which is analogous to our situation. There is no valid exegesis of what the prophets mean apart from what the prophets meant. Consequently, we must familiarize ourselves with the times in which the prophets lived and spoke. We must orient ourselves with the earlier material of the Old Testament to be able to recognize prophetic allusions to prior events and to catch their statements at a glance; otherwise, their oracles will remain a mystery to us. To follow any other procedure is actually a hanging upon the prophets that which one has accepted apart from the prophets. It is a proof texting which is sometimes called *isegesis* rather than *exegesis*.

The tension between "what it meant" and "what it means" is the most crucial issue in the question of current biblical exegesis. Scholarship seems able to reach a fair agreement on "what it meant." On the other hand, scholars are poles apart on "what it means."

At first thought one might feel that there should be no difference between these two points—once we determine what it meant, then that should be able to know what it means. But a second thought will show one that the prophets discussed sacrifice, fasting, and other topics which were duties under the Law but which are not duties for us at all. Threatened Assyrian or Babylonian invasions are not our concern. Furthermore, the passage of time may have revealed to us some things which were not yet clear to the prophets. The ultimate meaning of a prophecy cannot be understood apart from its fulfillment. A classic example is Caiaphas' statement that it was expedient that one man should die for the people (John 11:50-52; 18:14). The speaker intended only to state a political expediency. However, the full meaning of his statement can only be appreciated in the light of the biblical atonement. The one preparing the way (Mal. 3:1) and the Elijah to come (Mal. 4:5) become clear only with N.T. interpretation and with Jesus' application of the statement to John the Baptist (Matt. 17:12-13).

The Biblical Theology movement devoted great attention to the minute details of what the theologies of Isaiah, of Paul, of Peter, etc., were; but when the scholar had accomplished that, one could not assume that the personal beliefs and habits of that scholar would be closely related to what he had described. The procedure by which one moved from the description to current values was not always clear.

While hoping to avoid depicting the major prophets in his own image and to avoid treating their material as legal texts, the author hopes to make clear some prophetic values that by analogy are relevant for solving problems of twenty-first century living.

Questions for Discussion

1. Why the name "Major Prophets"?

2. What variety is seen in describing a prophet?

3. What sort of variety in literature is found in the Major Prophets?

4. At what period in Israel's history are the Major Prophets to be placed?

5. What external stimuli called forth Israel's prophets?

6. How is the book of Daniel different from the other Major Prophets?

7. How is the book of Lamentations different?

8. What makes Ezekiel distinctive?

9. What approaches to the prophets has the lesson suggested may be defective?

10. What stages can be traced out in Israel's prophetic movement?

Chapter II

THE CAREER OF THE PROPHET ISAIAH

Text Materials

The Qumran discoveries include twenty-one fragmentary manuscripts of the book of Isaiah. The Isaiah A scroll gives practically a complete text of Isaiah dating to the second century B.C., a thousand years older than any previously known text. Qumran has also supplied a fragment of a commentary on Isaiah (1QpIsa). There are also numerous citations of Isaiah in non-biblical Qumran documents (CD 4:12-18; 6:3-4; 7:10-12; 1QM 11:11-12). Isaiah is among the most frequently cited O.T. books in the New Testament. A fragment of Isaiah is in the Wadi Murabba'at materials (MurIsa). The major Greek codices from the 4th to 5th centuries A.D. include a Greek text of the book.

Isaiah is included in Ben Sira's survey of the great ones of the past with echoes of both halves of the book (Sir. 48:22-25). Qumran materials echo the second half of the book (4QTanh; 11QMelch 4, 15; CD 6:3-4) as well as the first (1QS 5:17-18; 4QFlor; CD 4:12-18; 7:10-12; 1QM 11:11-12). Josephus (*Ant.* 10:1.3 [11-35]) summarizes this period with allusions to Isaiah. *The Martyrdom of Isaiah* is conjecturally dated to the first century A.D.

The Vision of God

Chapter six of Isaiah's book is an excellent starting point for considering the career of Isaiah the son of Amoz. Narrating a vision from the year in which King Uzziah died (perhaps ca. 742 B.C. and shortly after the accession of Tiglath-pileser III of Assyria in 745 B.C.), the prophet tells how he is made aware of his own sinful state. The seraphs cry "Holy, holy, holy is the Lord God of Hosts." The prophet's most characteristic phrase to describe the Lord—a phrase found in his book twenty-nine times but found elsewhere in the Bible only six times—is "the Holy One of Israel." The impact of the concept of the holiness of

God influences the entire book. The Gospel of John alludes to Isaiah's seeing the glory of God (John 12:41).

The leprous person had to warn others by crying "Unclean, unclean" (Lev. 13:45). King Uzziah had become leprous by his presumption to burn incense in the temple (2 Chron. 26:16-21). Isaiah when seeing the Lord saw himself as a person of unclean lips (Isa. 6:5).

Despite Isaiah's fears, however, it is not for his doom that he has seen the Lord. It is the touch of the burning coal from the altar that cleanses him (Isa. 6:7). Out of it all, he volunteers for his task and receives his commission to preach. But it is a hopeless task on which he is sent. So far beyond the people's mental horizon was his message that they could not accept it. He must preach that God was fighting on the side of the Assyrians rather than on Israel's side. Judah, like all peoples at all times in war, counted God as one of its assets; but the prophet was to speak of God's strange deed (that of destruction) on Mount Zion; Isa. 28:21). The words of Isaiah are cited in Mark 4:11f. and Acts 28:26-27 to describe blindness to the Gospel.

In response to his query, "How long?" must this hopeless preaching go on, the reply is that it is until the land is waste and without inhabitant. But out of the whole destruction there is to be a stump left behind, and the holy seed is that stump. Here are three major elements stressed in the prophet's preaching: the calamity to come, the remnant to survive, and the future to grow out of it.

The Syro-Ephraimitic War

Isaiah fills the role of the advisor to the king. The first part of his book deals with five major episodes in which he was active. His career should be thought of in relation to these events. The first event is the Syro-Ephraimitic war of 734-732 B.C. (Isa. 7; 2 Kings 16:5).

Taking advantage of Assyria's involvement in the east, Aram, led by Rezin king of Damascus, and Israel, led by Pekah, plotted revolt against Assyria. When Ahaz, the young king of Judah, declined to join them, they besieged Jerusalem (2 Kings 15:37; 16:5) and planned to depose him and to put "the son of Tabeel" on the throne in his stead. The Philistines and Edomites annexed part of Judah's territory (2 Kings 16:6; 2 Chron. 28:1-18). The prospect of facing the two in battle scared

Ahaz so that "his heart . . . shook as the trees of the forest shake before the wind." The only recourse he could see was to hire Tiglath-pileser III of Assyria to invade his enemies from the rear and in that way to relieve the pressure on him (cf. 2 Kings 16:7; 2 Chron. 28:16).

While Ahaz was making plans for what seemed an inevitable siege, Isaiah was sent with his son "A Remnant Shall Return" to meet the king and to advise him to do nothing rash. The prophet insisted that the two opposing kings were only smoking tails of firebrands. Their power would soon be gone (cf. Isa. 7:7-8). Isaiah called on Ahaz to believe. He offered Ahaz any sign he would choose that his words were the truth; but the king, choosing refuge in lies (cf. Isa. 28:15), in feigned piety refused. He would not tempt God (cf. Deut. 6:16), he said. The prophet then returned that God would give a sign anyway. Within the time it takes a child to be born and before he could choose the good and refuse the evil (that is, within two or three years) the danger would have passed by.

But the prophet proceeded to point out that the policy being planned was completely disastrous. Ahaz was about to bring upon himself the king of Assyria—a problem greater than any faced since the division of the kingdom. In a series of figures, introduced four times by "in that day," the prophet described the crisis. The Assyrians are like a swarm of flies or bees which come and cover the whole land. The king of Assyria will give Ahaz a clean shave, removing not only the hair of the head and of the beard, but also the pubic hair. The calamity will be so severe that a cow and two sheep can supply the needs of the surviving remnant. Where there was previously a valuable, producing vineyard one will need protection to enter, and the vineyard is turned back to pasture.

Ahaz was not convinced by Isaiah. He went ahead with his plans, went to Damascus, and paid his tribute to Tiglath-pileser (2 Kings 16:5ff.). Assyrian records as well as the Old Testament note the tribute. The Assyrians attacked, captured Damascus, killed Rezin, and carried off the trans-Jordan and northern parts of Israel. Judah passed under Assyrian domination never again in the Old Testament period to gain her independence. Isaiah's threat had come to fruition; the future had been traded for relief in the present. The Chronicler comments that Tiglath-pileser afflicted Ahaz instead of strengthening him (2 Chron. 28:20).

The Sign

This story in chapter 7 is simple and straight forward enough were it not for verse fourteen. What is the sign the prophet speaks of? Tertullian in the second century set the pattern for later Christian thinking by affirming that in this case the event spoken of must be miraculous and unparalleled. The English reader automatically responds fallaciously, "a sign must be a miracle." But while in Hebrew a sign (*'oth*) may be a miracle, it is not necessarily one. It may be an ordinary event to which special significance is attached. Isaiah and his family are signs (Isa. 8:18). Isaiah's going naked and barefoot is a sign (Isa. 20:3). The sign to Hezekiah of his deliverance is "this year eat what grows of itself, and in the second year what springs of the same; then in the third year sow and reap, and plant vineyards, and eat of their fruit" (Isa. 37:30). In this last case, the passage of time or a span of time is a sign. In three seasons things would be back to normal.

In analogy with this last passage, the sign to Ahaz (Isa. 7:14) is that in the time it takes a child to be born and to learn to choose the good and refuse evil, the danger Ahaz fears will have passed by. Micah also uses childbirth as a measure of time (Mic. 5:[2]3). In other words, the basic message of Isa. 7:14 is parallel to that of Isa. 8:4 where essentially the same statement is made about the prophet's child in measuring time.

The 'Almah

'Almah (under the influence of Matt. 1:23 traditionally translated "virgin" in Isa. 7:14) is a feminine form from a Hebrew root meaning to be mature and can rightly be translated "young woman." A part of the dispute over this term comes from the fact that older lexicographers attempted to derive the word from a root which to them meant to seclude. This idea continues to influence the uninformed person long after it has been abandoned by the experts in Hebrew language. The masculine form 'elem (translated "youth") of the same root as 'almah occurs in 1 Sam. 17:56 and 20:22 where no one argues that sexual experience or lack of it is being considered. The masculine form describes the young human male, and the feminine as its counterpart should describe the young human female. Lad and lassie are comparable terms in English. The feminine form 'almah occurs in seven Old Testament passages (Gen. 24:43; Exod. 2:8; Ps. 68:26; Prov. 30:19; Song 1:3; 6:8; Isa. 7:14). Neither the ancient versions nor the English versions have consistently used "virgin" for the translation of all of these passages.

While *bethulah* is used in the Old Testament legal passages where technical virginity is under discussion (Exod. 22:[15]16; cf. Deut. 22:19), an 'almah can also be a *bethulah*. To recognize that 'almah means a young adult female is not to deny virgin birth interpretation of the passage as given in Matthew. A young woman in English usage may also be a virgin. Genesis 24:16, 43 makes this matter clear when the same woman—Rebecca—is described with both words (*bethulah* and 'almah). The other Old Testament passages are actually ambiguous on the issue of virginity and are not primarily discussing the woman's sexual status. One cannot prove that the individuals were not virgins in the technical sense, but need they be? The discussion on the meaning of this root has now shifted to its use in the Aramaic version (where 'almah describes a woman no longer a virgin; Judg. 19:3); and to its use in the cognate Semitic languages.

Certainly Isaiah was not predicting a virgin birth to take place in his own day. There was only one virgin birth in history. If a birth took place in Isaiah's day it must have been an ordinary one to which the significance we have above described was attached—that is, to the time involved. That is, Isaiah was using the birth and development process as a known measure of time.

Actually, the only major question concerning Isa. 7:14 is that of how Matthew interprets the passage when he informs us that it predicts the virgin birth of Jesus. Matthew uses what we call "typical" fulfillment when he applies "Out of Egypt have I called my son" (Matt. 2:15; cf. Hos. 11:1) and "Rachel weeping for her children" (Matt. 2:18; cf. Jer. 31:15) both of which in their Old Testament setting describe Old Testament events. For the person who accepts the Gospel of Matthew, this must needs be a legitimate interpretation. Though we may debate over whether or not Matthew is also interpreting Isa. 7:14 in the same way, there is no compelling reason to eliminate the possibility from consideration. The sign of Ahaz was the span of time involved in the

Jack P. Lewis

birth of a child and his coming to the age of discretion.

A unique event to happen 735 years later—though most significant to me—would not have solved the problem of a king who already disbelieved the promise the prophet has made him. He could not wait 735 years to see what the truth was. He must act and take the consequences of his choice.

Immanuel, the name given to the child, also deserves consideration. The name means "God is with us." The idea, but not as a proper name, also occurs in Isa. 8:10. Immanuel is addressed concerning the Assyrian invasion as though he were a contemporary figure (Isa. 8:6). Names of the type in which God is said to do something (e.g. Samuel, Zedekiah, Joshua) need not imply that the possessor is divine. The Italian ruler Victor Immanuel was not thought to be divine. American parents also name sons "Manuel." It is likely here also in citing Isa. 7:14 that Matthew informs us that there is a deeper significance in the name than would have been obvious in Isaiah's day when a child was so named. That child was named as a token of the deliverance—"God is with us," "God was with us," or "God be with us"—but is not himself represented as the deliverer. Without question, in Matthew's interpretation the possessor of the name is divine. Prophecies can be reinterpreted. Caiaphas' prophecy that it was expedient that one man die for the people and not that the whole people perish had a significance of which he never dreamed (John 11:50-52; 18:14).

A Hebrew bulla (made in clay by a stamp seal) has been recently published by N. Avigad which has the name *'Immadiyahu* which means "The Lord is with me." This sort of name also occurs with a Baal element in the name Ittobaal ("Baal is with him"; cf. "Ethbaal"; 1 Kings 16:31) which is found on the Ahiram sarcophagus. The publisher of the bulla calls our attention to the fact that a parallel was also found in the Elephantine papyri in the name *'Immanuiah* meaning "Yahweh is with us." Also, Avigad, modifying the vocalization earlier proposed by its excavator, notices that a list of names found at Horvat 'Uza in the Negeb has the name *'mdyhw bn zkr* which would be "Immadiyahu son of Zakkur." The only differences between these names and that used by Isa. 7:14 are that they have the divine element "Yahweh" instead of "El" in them, and two of them have the first person pronoun instead of the second. The declaration of faith is the same in them all. These names make it likely that a child could have been named "Immanuel" in Isaiah's day, with the time lapse between his conception, birth, and learning to make choices as the sign of which Isaiah spoke.

God being with Israel is not an unusual O.T. concept. It is stated in several O.T. passages (Josh. 1:5; Ps. 23:4; 46:7, 11; Isa. 8:10; cf. Amos 5:14). Isa. 7:14 is not the only place where Isaiah uses childbirth as an image. Hezekiah describes the situation in which he is, "Children have come to the birth, and there is no strength to bring them forth" (Isa. 37:3).

The argument that has been made is not intended to challenge the interpretation of "Immanuel" made in the Gospel of Matthew (Matt. 1:23) which obviously refers to the incarnation. Matthew in the birth narratives informs the reader that there is fulfillment which would not have been obvious to the first reader of prophetic statements (cf. Matt. 2:15, 18).

The Assyrian Commander in Chief at Ashdod (Isa. 20)

The years of Isaiah's career passed swiftly by; kings changed in Assyria as Tiglath-pileser III gave way to Shalmaneser V, and he to Sargon II. Israel went into its exile in 722 B.C.; and in Judah, Ahaz was replaced by Hezekiah in 715 B.C. Since Isaiah's oracles are undated, it is not possible to assign them to specific events of these years and in that way to trace out Isaiah's career. By about 712 B.C., the Philistine area was seething with revolt against Assyria. Rulers changed in the region but international policies remained the same across the period of history. To gain their freedom from Assyria (or later from Babylon), the Judeans sought the aid of Egypt.

The possibility that Hezekiah would be drawn into the revolt was real, and so in the year that the Tartan (the commander-in-chief) of Sargon came to Ashdod to quell the revolt, Isaiah was commissioned by the Lord to go naked and barefoot (Isa. 20:2). Nudity was considered scandalous in Israel (Gen. 9:2ff.; 2 Sam. 6:20). For three years he was a walking sign against Egypt and Ethiopia. The Egyptians and Ethiopians would be led off captive in this pathetic condition. How then could they furnish help? The oracle against Ethiopia (Isa. 18) may fit this period. See also the oracle on Philistia in Isa. 14:28-31 though it is dated earlier.

Evidently Isaiah's action was effective for we have no evidence when the revolt was stamped out that reprisals were taken by the Assyrians against Hezekiah as we would expect had he been involved.

In 1843, Paul Emile Botta discovered the palace of Sargon at Khorsabad and in the palace found Sargon's own account of the revolt and of the Ashdod campaign in two different documents ($ANET^3$, 287a). More recently in the excavations at Ashdod itself fragments of a basalt stele set up there by the Assyrians were discovered. These form one of the most striking direct contacts between archaeological material and a biblical event.

Hezekiah's Illness (Isa. 38:1-22; 2 Kings 20:1-11)

Sometime near the end of the eighth century Hezekiah was desperately ill. The illness must have been before the defeat of Sennacherib for at the end of the affair God promises Hezekiah that he will deliver him from the Assyrians and defend the city (Isa. 38:6). One need not assume that events are narrated in the prophetic books in chronological order. Jeremiah dates many of his oracles, but they are not arranged in a chronological order. Isaiah upon this occasion of Hezekiah's illness calls upon the king to arrange his affairs in view of his immediately approaching death. In deep humility, Hezekiah turned his face to the wall and prayed to the Lord. The prophet was sent back to announce that the prayer had been heard; that fifteen years had been added to the king's life; and that the city would be spared from the Assyrians. When offered a sign, the king chose that of the shadow turning back ten steps on the dial of Ahaz. The king set forth a psalm of praise for his recovery (Isa. 38:15-20).

Merodach-baladan (Isa. 39:1-8; 2 Kings 20:12-19)

It is not possible to know the chronological sequence concerning Sennacherib's invasion and the embassy of Merodach-baladan. We know from non-biblical sources that this figure was a thorn in the side to the four Assyrian rulers from Tiglath-pileser III to Sennacherib. The book of Isaiah, as the book of Kings, suggests that Merodach-baladan's messengers came to congratulate Hezekiah upon his recovery from illness. 2 Chron. 32:31 suggests that they came to inquire about the sign that had been given which interrupted time. Josephus (*Ant.* 10.2.2 [30ff.]) suggests (on what evidence is unknown) they hoped to enlist Hezekiah in their planned revolt against Assyria. While Hezekiah showed them all his treasures, Isaiah took an extremely dim view of the whole affair and threatened that the entire treasure as well as some of Hezekiah's sons would be taken to Babylon. This is the one prediction of Babylonian captivity by the prophet Isaiah though there are echoes of the captivity in the oracles against Babylon. Faced with this threat, Hezekiah, caught in the act, could only be grateful that the consequences would have to be faced by others rather than by himself.

Sennacherib's Invasion (Isa. 36-37; 2 Kings 18:13ff.)

All the threats which the prophets had made of an Assyrian invasion of Judah came to tragic fulfillment with Sennacherib's invasion of 701 B.C. The affair is narrated both in the Bible and in Sennacherib's own records. In copies on at least three objects (the Taylor prism, the Baghdad prism, and on the winged bulls) Sennacherib tells how Hezekiah was drawn into the intrigue of the Philistine states; how the Assyrians came to Lachish, how Sennacherib took forty-six of Hezekiah's walled cities and many villages, and how he shut him up like a bird in a cage in his city of Jerusalem. A large wall picture found in thirteen slabs in the excavation of Sennacherib's palace at Nineveh, but now in the British Museum, shows the king seated on his throne with the spoil of Lachish being carried before him.

Isaiah dates the invasion in the fourteenth year of Hezekiah and tells how the Assyrian official, the Rabshakeh, came from Lachish to Jerusalem to make his demands on Hezekiah. While parleying with the Judean officials, the commander called their plans for defense mere words. Should they hope to get help from Egypt, Egypt was a broken reed of a staff which would pierce the one who leans on it. He suggested that Hezekiah's reform had angered the Lord rather than pleased him. He offered to furnish horses for a mock battle if they wanted to fight even one captain of Assyria—not to mention the whole Assyrian army. He also claimed a divine commission to destroy the land (Isa. 36:1-10). Meanwhile, Hezekiah was encouraging his people (2 Chron. 32:7-8).

In an effort to demoralize the Judean people, the Rabshakeh insists that Hezekiah is causing them to hope falsely in the Lord. He suggests that exile is not such a bad fate after all. He points out that other gods have been unable to deliver their people.

In utter helplessness Hezekiah beseeched the Lord in the temple. When Isaiah was consulted, he assured the servants of Hezekiah that the Assyrian would withdraw. But the withdrawal was not before Hezekiah had paid a heavy tribute (2 Kings 18:13-16).

However, Hezekiah's tribute did not satisfy Sennacherib. Having left Lachish and having come to Libnah which is nearer Jerusalem, Sennacherib heard of planned aid to Hezekiah from Tirhakah of Ethiopia. Consequently, he again demanded Hezekiah's surrender. This time the main thrust of his persuasion was that other gods had not delivered their people from Assyria; hence, he suggests that hope in the Lord is vain.

Hezekiah spread the letter before the Lord in the temple and the Lord heard the king's prayer. The Assyrian in his blasphemy had over-bid his hand. Isaiah was commissioned to give king Hezekiah assurance that the army would not enter Jerusalem.

By a stroke of the Lord, 185,000 soldiers died in the night, and Sennacherib had to withdraw never to return. Some twenty years later Sennacherib was murdered by his sons (Isa. 37:36-38). Isaiah summarizes the crisis of 701:

> At evening time, behold terror!

> Before morning they are no more (Isa. 17:14).

Byron celebrated the event with his "The Destruction of Sennacherib":

> The might of the Gentile, unsmote by the sword,

> Hath melted like snow in the glance of the Lord!

Conclusion

These events in the clash of Judah with Assyria are those of the years of Isaiah's career. The Bible has no information on later years of the prophet's life. The Pseudepigrapha gives a legend of his being sawn asunder by king Manasseh. It is in connection with the Assyrian danger that the warnings of the first part of Isaiah's book are to be interpreted. The calamity predicted in the prophet's call (Isa. 6) was experienced. A remnant had survived.

Questions for Discussion

1. What is most significant of Isaiah's vision of the Lord?

2. What was confusing about Isaiah's preaching?

3. Are there non-miraculous signs in Scripture?

4. Is the word *'almah* unique to Isaiah 7:14?

5. What unusual contact is there between archaeological finds and the book of Isaiah? (Birth of Jesus)

6. What unusual miracle is narrated in the book of Isaiah?

7. What is the main focal point of the threats made in the book of Isaiah?

8. How did Judah come under the domination of Assyria?

9. How did Isaiah characterize Ahaz's plans?

10. What light has been shed on use of the name Immanuel?

Chapter III

GOD OR EGYPT?

The Song of the Vineyard (Isa. 5:1ff.)

The situation in Judah which brought on her doom is graphically presented by Isaiah in his allegory, the Song of the Vineyard. By telling an apparently innocent story about grape culture (one of the main agricultural activities of Palestine), the prophet traps the audience by their answer to his question into convicting themselves. This procedure is like that earlier followed by Nathan in his story of the lamb (2 Sam. 12:1ff.), by the wise woman of Tekoa in her story of her fighting sons (2 Sam. 14:5ff.), and by the unnamed prophet with his story of the escaped prisoner (1 Kings 20:39-42).

What should be done with a vineyard that after all diligent care produced only wild grapes? The vineyard could only be abandoned and turned back to the pasture. But the point of the prophet is that Judah and Israel are the vineyard of the Lord (cf. Jer. 2:21; Ezek. 15:1ff.; Hos. 10:1; John 15). In puns, which translators do not attempt in English, he points out that where God expected justice (*mishpat*) there was bloodshed (*mishpak*) and for righteousness (*tsedhakhah*) there was only the cry (*tsa'akhah*) of the oppressed. Isaiah had described Jerualsm as having been in the past a city of righteousness (*tsedheq*; Isa. 1:21-27). Opportunity had brought responsibility, but Judah had been found wanting.

The Wild Grapes of Judah

Isaiah makes a frontal attack on Judah's pride which is to be brought low. Isaiah uses the phrase "day of the Lord" twice (Isa. 2:12; 13:6). The Lord has "a day" against all that is haughty. Isaiah lists symbols of what is high: cedars of Lebanon, oaks of Bashan, high mountains, fortified walls, and ships of Tarshish. In the end only the Lord will be exalted (Isa. 2:12-17).

The leaders are blamed for the delinquency (Isa. 3:1-15). Isaiah can call them "rulers of Sodom" (Isa. 1:10). The rulers will be carried off and will be replaced.

Like other prophets of the 8th century, Isaiah has much to say about the oppression of the poor. He denounces the fashionable women of Zion who in their finery parade themselves (Isa. 3:16ff.). After giving an extended list of what a well-dressed lady of the eighth century would wear, he reminds them that captives' garb awaits them. Their men are destined for the sword while they themselves are destined to be raped by the enemy (Isa. 3:17-26). In the imbalance of the sexes following the war, seven women will be willing to share one husband and furnish their own support (Isa. 4:1ff.) which in Israelite culture a husband was obligated to furnish (Exod. 21:10-11). The prophet is not speaking either of a condition in heaven or of a millennial sort of period in which men will have a Morman type heaven of multiple wives, but he speaks of the consequences of war. It is unfortunate that the chapter division separates this last section from its context in the preceding chapter. In a later oracle the prophet again threatens the women, telling them that they have little more than a year before the calamity strikes (Isa. 32:9-10).

Some of the sins of Judah are to be seen in Isaiah's series of seven woes. First there are the land grabbers who add field to field, doubtless ignoring the needs of the poor (Isa. 5:8f.). Micah 3:1ff. offers a parallel. Driven off the land, a person could only go into slavery. There are the drunkards and revelers who refuse to face up to the fate which the Lord is bringing (Isa. 5:11-12). There are the skeptical who say they will believe the prophet's threats only after the threats have been accomplished (Isa. 5:18-19). There are those of perverted standards who call evil good and good evil (Isa. 5:20). There are those who are wise in their own eyes (Isa. 5:21). There are those who are brave in facing a highball but who do not reject a bribe when it is offered (Isa. 5:22). Finally there are those who make unjust laws in order to oppress the poor (Isa. 10:1). Defeat in battle and exile stare all these people in the face.

Idolatry is prominent in the sins Isaiah denounced (Isa. 2:8, 18, 20). Another series of sins is to be seen in the group of five which ends "For all this his anger is not turned away and his hand is stretched out still" (Isa. 5:25; 9:12-10:4). The phrase is an inversion of the one describing the hand of the Lord that had delivered Israel from Egypt (Exod. 13:14, 16; Deut. 5:15; 6:21; 7:8; 9:26; 26:8).

The Rod of God's Anger

Because of all Israel's sins, God has a day against all that is proud and lofty (Isa. 2:12-22). The stupefying message which Isaiah was commissioned to preach (Isa. 6:9) was that God was fighting on the side of the Assyrians—not on the side of Judah. Such an idea was beyond the mental grasp of his audience. Judah, like all other people, counted God as one of their assets. They were told of God's "strange work" (Isa. 28:21); they heard, but were only stupefied. Another of Isaiah's figures compares them to a people who are frustrated by a sealed book, but who, even when the book is open, cannot read (Isa. 29:11-12). Isaiah insists that God signals for a nation afar off to come. Like lions the enemy carries off prey and none can rescue (Isa. 5:26ff.).

Surely among the most striking of the prophet's oracles is his declaration that Assyria is the rod of God's anger sent against Judah who is called a godless nation (Isa. 10:5ff.). Assyria is, of course, an unconscious servant of the Lord, bent only on carrying on aggressive war and grabbing what land she can. She boasts in her strength which enables her to spoil nations as easily as one robs a bird's nest.

But when the Lord has finished his work on Mount Zion, he will punish Assyria who really is merely as an axe or a saw in his hand. Assyria's army will be destroyed. Using the figure of trees of a forest, the prophet insists that the remnant will be so few that even a child can write the number down. One of the great ideas of Isaiah is that God uses nations for his purpose.

However, the ultimate fate in store for Assyria should not hide the fact that now Judah must face Assyria. Graphically the prophet envisions the approach of the enemy to the city of Jerusalem (Isa. 10:28-32). It is no Armageddon battle at the end of days that he is describing. Scofield erroneously assigns this description to the approach and destruction of the Gentile hosts under the Beast for which he appeals to Dan. 17:8; Rev. 19:20. But actually, Assyria in the eighth century B.C. was knocking on the door.

Jack P. Lewis

25

It is not possible to know specifically the occasion of the prophet's "oracle concerning the valley of vision" (Isa. 22). It has been suggested that it was either upon the completion of the alliance with Egypt or upon the departure of the Assyrian representative when Hezekiah had paid his tribute to Sennacherib. At any rate, the contrast is between the people's vision and the prophet's vision. They have broken out in wild victory type celebration, but the prophet turns aside to weep over the destruction of his people. The valleys are full of the enemy. The people have examined the preparedness of the weapons (Isa. 22:8-11) but have not considered that their real problem is in their relation to the Lord. When there is need for sackcloth, they are saying, "Let us eat, drink and be merry."

The particular cause of the prophet's severe denunciation of Shebna, the prime minister ("who is over the house"), is unknown. It has been suggested that Shebna was the leader of the pro-Egyptian party. The prophet finds him carving a tomb for himself and announces his removal from office. He will be replaced by Eliakim who will then bear the authority (Isa. 22:15ff.). A rock-cut tomb from this period found in the Silvan village has an obliterated name, but has the title "who is over the house." It has been suggested that it could be Shebna's tomb, but in the absence of a name, the suggestion can be no more than a conjecture. In Isa. 36:3; 37:2, in the negotiations with the Assyrians, Eliakim is "over the household" and Shebna is only the secretary. Presumably the change Isaiah threatened had taken place.

Line upon Line (28:1ff.)

Very little of Isaiah seems addressed to the northern kingdom. The prophet seems to have surprised a crowd at a drunken party at which time he set forth his woe upon the drunkards of Ephraim, the northern people. They are really like fading flowers which revelers wear upon their heads at a party; however, the carousing is about over.

The drunkards seem to retort to the prophet either in baby talk or in drunkards' prattle as they characterize his work as that of teaching infants who prattle out unintelligible phrases. The English Bible, attempting to make sense of these words, translates them as "line upon line; precept upon precept," a statement which some have twisted into a description of the method of God's revelation.

The prophet takes up their challenge. God will indeed teach them by foreign talk which will be as unintelligible as the prattle they have thrown out. They insist that their plans are adequate to deal with the situation. They have a covenant (doubtless an alliance with Egypt) with death so that the danger will not reach them. The prophet assures them their covenant will not stand. Not only so, but should they grasp what he is really saying, "it would be sheer terror to understand." In one of his most classic comparisons, the prophet characterizes their plans as a bed too short to stretch out on and covers too narrow to wrap oneself in.

The Lord has acted at other times—for example at Baal- perazim where David won a victory over the Philistines (2 Sam. 5:20ff.) and at Gibeon where Joshua defeated the kings at the conquest (Josh. 10:1ff.)—only this time it is a strange work he does. As the farmer varies his agricultural activities with the season, the Lord can change his action. He need not help Israel all the time. He can rise up to aid the enemy. He will encamp against Jerusalem (Isa. 28:1-29).

The Broken Reed of a Staff

The international policy of the kings of Judah seems always to have been constant. By securing the aid of Egypt which supplied horses and chariots, they hoped to gain their independence from Assyria during the Assyrian period and from Babylon during the Babylonian period a century later. Such a policy spelled tragedy to Isaiah. With a great deal of descriptive power, Isaiah describes rebellious children who carry out a plan that is not the Lord's. They load their treasures on donkeys and camels to carry them through the desert "to a people that cannot help them. Egypt's help is worthless and empty, therefore I have called her Rahab who sits still" (Isa. 30:6-7). A further woe is upon those who go to Egypt for help and rely on horses and chariots (Isa. 31:1ff.). The prophet insists, "The Egyptians are men, and not God; their horses are flesh and not spirit" (Isa. 31:3). Isaiah's oracles on foreign nations include an oracle on both Ethiopia and Egypt (Isa. 18-19).

The Alternative to Futility: What God Wants (Isa. 1)

Isaiah begins his book with a charge against his people that their behavior has been unnatural. The ox and the donkey know their master, but Judah does not know God. He compares them to a person who has been beaten until no sound place is left (Isa. 1:5-6). The country has been defeated in war so that only a remnant is left (Isa. 1:7-9).

The people's response was to suppose that additional sacrifice, observance of festivals, and prayer would placate the Lord (Isa. 1:10-12). Calling his people people of Sodom and Gomorrah, Isaiah, like most of the prophets, insists that in the face of their danger it is not sacrifice that God demands. With sacrifices and festivals God is weary (Isa. 1:11ff.) These statements are doubtless to be taken in a comparative way. In Judah's situation sacrifice could not help her. Repentance was that which was really needed.

Isaiah's message is essentially a call to repentance. Describing a nation invaded in which there are only a few survivors (Isa. 1:7-9), he calls upon them to cease to do evil and to correct oppression (Isa. 1:16-17). The Lord wants right treatment of fellow-man. External acts of worship are worthless when not accompanied by mercy to fellowmen.

Jerusalem has departed from justice; the princes are rebels; all love bribes. Only a complete about face can save her. In addition to her injustice she has also her sacred idolatrous gardens, but all is doomed to fire.

Only repentance and obedience can bring safety. Sins like scarlet can be white as snow (Isa. 1:18-19). But if the people refuse, they face the sword (Isa. 1:20).

Isaiah promises:

> Turn to him from whom you have deeply revolted, O people of Israel. For in that day every one shall cast away his idols of silver and his idols of gold, which your hands have sinfully made for you. "And the Assyrian shall fall by a sword, not of man; and a sword, not of man, shall devour him; and he shall flee from the sword, and his young men shall be put to forced labor. His rock shall pass away in terror, and his officers desert the standard in panic," says the Lord (Isa. 31:6-9).

The Oracles on Foreign Nations

The books of the prophets often contain three elements: oracles of condemnation for his own people, oracles of doom on foreign nations (Amos 1-2; Jer. 46-51; Ezek. 25-32), and oracles of hope. In this lesson we give attention to oracles on foreign nations in the book of Isaiah which occupy chs. 13-19; 21; 23; 34. In these oracles eight nations: Babylon, Philistia, Moab, Damascus, Ethiopia, Egypt, Dumah, and Arabia are dealt with. Each (except concerning Ethiopia [Isa. 18:1]) is introduced with the technical word *masa'* sometimes translated "burden" on the assumption that it comes from the root *nasa'* "to lift up"; but which technically means "an oracle of doom." The term may come from the fact that one lifts his hand in a solemn oath (Ps. 106:26) or lifts up his voice. The word occurs ten times at the head of sections in chapters 13-23. Those dealing with foreign nations will be considered here in the order in which they are arranged in the book of Isaiah.

Babylon. The Lord "from the bare mountain" (a point of vantage for signaling) summons the nations as a consecrated army to muster to attack Babylon. This attack is "the day of the Lord" for Babylon in the face of which her people are helpless as a woman in childbirth (Isa. 13:6-8). In poetic figures of speech, even the heavens refuse Babylon their light (Isa. 13:10). Men flee right and left; life is considered as worthless (Isa. 13:14-16). The Medes, who cannot be bought off, are the Lord's agents in the destruction, and Babylon is left as desolate as Sodom and Gomorrah (Isa. 13:17-22). The time is at hand. Babylon's crimes are not detailed, but vaguely include "evil,' "iniquity," "pride," and "haughtiness" (Isa. 13:11, 19).

A second section dealing with Babylon is a taunt (*mashal*), cast in the dirge meter, against the fallen king of Babylon (Isa. 14:4ff.). With his fall the oppressed earth, its inhabitants, and the cedars of Lebanon break forth in singing (Isa. 14:5-8). Even Sheol stirs itself to meet the king as he comes down. Here we find one of the most detailed descriptions of conditions in Sheol to be found in the Bible, but see also Job 3:1ff.. The inhabitants, formerly rulers of earth, are shades (*repha'im*) who rise from their thrones to express surprise that the king of Babylon has become as weak as they (Isa. 14:9-11).

In the taunt, the king is called "morning star (*heosphoros*)" in the Septuagint, in the NRSV "Day Star, son of Dawn," in the NIV "morning star, son of the dawn," but in the KJV is "Lucifer, son of the morning." This latter translation from Latin (where Lucifer meant "morning star) gives us one of the popular names for the devil and is the only occurrence of the name in Scripture. Some church fathers, connecting this passage erroneously with Luke 10:18, referred the passage to the fall of Satan, and this passage through Milton's *Paradise Lost* has exercised great influence on popular notions of the origin of the devil. Any fair reading of this passage in its context, however, should convince one that it is not dealing with the devil and his origin.

The king who thought to exalt himself to being God's equal has been brought down to Sheol or to the Pit (*bor*). This last term is an alternate Old Testament name for the realm of the dead. The king's fate is the opposite of that which he expected as he lies unburied and trodden under foot of men (Isa. 14:12-21). Helpful material on the history of Babylon may be found in A. Parrot, *Babylon and the Old Testament* (London: S.C.M. Press, 1958) and in Gerald A. Larue, *Babylon and the Bible* (Grand Rapids: Baker, 1969). The prophet turns attention again to Babylon in ch. 21 which oracle will be considered in its proper sequence.

Assyria. Only a few verses (Isa. 14:24-27) threaten the downfall of Assyria. The Lord's purpose is to break Assyria in his land. The hand of the Lord is stretched out. None can turn it back.

Philistia. The oracle on Philistia is unlike all the other of Isaiah's oracles on foreign nations in that a specific date is attached to it—the year that King Ahaz died, or *ca.* 727 B.C. Tiglath-pileser III also died in the same year. Other chronologies may give the date of Ahaz's death at 717. It is one of the few dated oracles of the book of Isaiah (cf. Isa. 6:1; 36:1). At the prospects of throwing off the yolk of Assyria, Philistia is rejoicing—likely at the death of an Assyrian ruler, but is cautioned by the prophet that rejoicing is premature. Worse oppression is in store as a danger out of the north advances in whose ranks there is no straggler (Isa. 14:28-31). Shalmaneser V followed hard on the heels of Tiglath-pileser III, he by Sargon II, and Sargon II was followed by Sennacherib. Judah is advised to join in no such revolts (Isa. 14:32). Her protection is in the Lord and not in worldly alliances.

Moab. The Moabite peoples, descendants of Lot (Gen. 19:37), occupied a territory east of the Dead Sea between the river Arnon (Wadi

Mojib) and the brook Zered (Wadi-el Hesa); however, in this oracle some cities further to the north, namely, Nebo, Madeba, and Dibon, are dealt with. The Moabite stone (now at the Louvre museum) containing Mesha king of Moab's account of the conflicts with Israelite kings (cf. 1 Kings 3) is the chief remaining monument of Moab.

Sympathy is expressed for the complete destruction as the daughter of Moab goes up to the high places to weep (Isa. 15:1-9). Messengers are sent to Zion asking refuge for fugitives (Isa. 16:1-5), but the request is refused (Isa. 16:6-7). It is promised that in three short years the fate of Moab will be experienced (Isa, 16:13-14). This oracle should be compared with that of Jeremiah 48 and of Zephaniah 2:8 which are closely related to it.

Damascus. Damascus, chief city of the Aramean state in the area which later became Syria, was in constant conflict with Israel during the period of the divided kingdom. Damascus is threatened with total ruin. Its fate is presented in marked contrast with the remnant that is to be left to Israel (Isa. 17:1ff.). Damascus suffered in 734 B.C. at the hands of Tiglath-pileser III and is not further mentioned as an independent state in the Old Testament. This oracle should be read against the background of chs. 7-8 which we have studied earlier.

Ethiopia. Ethiopia, a land of insects, sends its messengers by the Nile in papyrus vessels, perhaps to make alliances (Isa. 18:1ff.). The prophet, in a figure which compares the situation to a harvest which will surely come, threatens that the people of Ethiopia will be left as prey to birds of the mountains and to beasts of the earth. Eventually Ethiopia will bring gifts to the Lord at Mount Zion (Isa. 18:6-7). Nations brought gifts to Hezekiah when Sennacherib withdrew (2 Chron. 32:23).

Egypt. The Lord comes to Egypt, civil war breaks out, and Egypt is given over to foreign domination (Isa. 19:1ff.). Its fate is described as a stroke against the Nile, Egypt's life stream. Isaiah is against any alliances. The princes of Egypt are declared to be fools. This oracle is particularly interesting in view of the standing Judean hope of aid from Egypt. Egypt was conquered by Esarhaddon in 670 B.C. and later by Ashurbanipal in 663 B.C.

The prophet seems to envision a conversion of Egypt to the worship of the Lord and a division of power with Israel, Egypt, and Assyria (Isa. 19:23-24). Chapter 20 is a further graphic warning of the outcome of Egyptian plotting. The captive's garb awaited her.

The Wilderness of the Sea. It would seem that the prophet returns to Babylon a second time in his "oracle concerning the wilderness of the sea" (Isa. 21:1-10). It is a message of terror that makes him reel to contemplate. The Lord charges him to set a watchman to look for messengers coming to announce the fall of Babylon. This oracle, like the two that follow, is characterized by an expression of sympathy for the conquered nation. The prophet's cry: "Fallen, fallen is Babylon" is later taken up in Rev. 18:2 with an allegorical interpretation.

Dumah. Dumah (the Septuagint version had Idumea) is Edom with the first letter shifted to the end as children do in words of pig Latin (Isa. 21:11-12). The watchman is asked, "What of the night?" The answer is unclear, but seems to hold no hope for Edom. One conquest of her (Assyria, Babylon, Persia, Greece, and Rome) led to another. The inquirer is invited to ask again.

If we are correct in identifying Dumah with Edom, then the same people are further dealt with in ch. 34. Edom is the subject of a violent outpouring of the wrath of God. Sacrificial imagery plays a great part in the picture. The Lord is the sacrificer and Edom is the victim sacrificed. Edom falls to rise no more. Her land is to be a land of perpetual burnings and of solitude. Its name is "No Kingdom There" (Isa. 34:12). There is a further oracle on Edom in ch. 63 where a warrior comes with the blood of divine vengeance besprinkled upon him.

Arabia. The caravans of Dedan have by war been driven off their accustomed routes of trade (Isa. 21:13-17). They appeal to the people of Tema (located halfway between Damascus and Mecca) for food and water. The threat of the prophet is that in one year their fate will be sealed.

Tyre. Tyre and Sidon, cities of the Phoenicians renowned for their trade, are called to wailing (Isa. 23:1-18). Their fate is sad news to Egypt, for the trade of Tyre has benefitted many lands. Her fall is the purpose of the Lord of hosts, and the Chaldeans seem to be the agents. After a desolation of seventy years (compare the exile of Judah [Jer. 25:11]), Tyre is to be rebuilt and will enrich the temple (Isa. 23:17-18).

The picture of Tyre as the harlot has influenced the imagery of Rev. 17:2. Phoenicia was invaded by Assyria twice in Isaiah's day: first by Shalmaneser V (727-722 B.C) and second by Sennacherib in his 701 B.C. campaign. Nebuchadnezzar besieged Tyre in vain (572 B.C.), but it was taken by Alexander the Great (332 B.C.).

The oracles on foreign nations denounce pride and teach that the heathen as well as Judah are responsible to the Lord and may, if they wish, share in his mercy and grace.

Questions for Discussion

1. What is the point of Isaiah's Song of the Vineyard?

2. What were some of Judah's prominent sins?

3. What role does Assyria play as seen by Isaiah?

4. How does Isaiah's vision differ from that of his audience?

5. What encounter did Isaiah have with Shebna?

6. What encounter did Isaiah have with drunkards?

7. How does Isaiah see Egypt?

8. What alternative does Isaiah hold out for Judah?

9. What is the Lord's work as described by Isaiah?

10. What similarities can be seen between life in Isaiah's time and the modern age?

Chapter IV

THE EXILE IS OVER

Isaiah 40-66

It is obvious, even to the casual reader, that the subject matter and the historical background of Isa. 40-66 are markedly different from those of chapters 1-39. The first part of the book, centering upon the clash with Assyria which reached its zenith in the invasion of Sennacherib in 701 B.C., deals with matters contemporary with Isaiah in the eighth century B.C. The second part of the book centers upon events that took place two hundred years later; namely, upon the return from Babylonian captivity accomplished by the rise to power of Cyrus, king of Persia. The first part of the book has only one prediction of Babylonian captivity (Isa. 39:6; cf. 2 Kings 20:17) but assumes the captivity in the oracles on Babylon (Isa. 13-14; 21:1-10). Neither Babylon nor Persia was a serious contender for domination of the Middle East in the days of Isaiah. In other words, a span of time as long as from the American Revolution to our own day separates the themes of the two parts of the book.

Following the lead of Bernhard Duhm (1892), critical circles universally argue that the two parts of the book have not been written by one author and consequently postulate a Second Isaiah as author for the second section. This second Isaiah is supposed to be a completely anonymous prophet of the Exile who was one of the major religious geniuses of all time, who had some of the world's most exalted religious ideas, and who first among Old Testament writers achieved pure monotheism. Apart from the hypothesis, however, this prophet with no name is completely unknown; history has no allusion to him. Some critics separate Isaiah 55-66 into yet another work called Third Isaiah (Trito-Isaiah).

A part of the argument for this division of the book is based upon the dogma accepted in critical prophetic study that a prophet speaks of events of his own day. Since the second part of the book speaks of things long after Isaiah's time, it is argued that the second part must be by someone else. The validity of the dogma is of course open to challenge. There are some contrary factors to consider.

The contention is about a stage of transmission of the text earlier than our first external evidence. Our oldest copy of Isaiah—the Dead Sea Scroll dating to the B.C. period—is a continuous text and indicates no consciousness on the part of the scribe of a break at the end of chapter 39. In the manuscript, chapter forty continues without a break. Jesus and writers of the New Testament cite both halves of the book and attribute the material to Isaiah (cf. Luke 4:17-19; John 12:38-41; Rom 9:27-29; 10:20-21). All other external evidence, such as that of the Septuagint version, Ecclesiasticus 48:22-25, Qumran materials (CD 6:8; 4QTan; 4QCatena[a]; 11QMelch 15), and Josephus (*Ant.* 11.1.2 [5]), also treats the book as a unified book.

Furthermore, while stressing dissimilarities in the style of writing of the two halves of the book, critics are forced to admit the similarity when making the postulated author to be a disciple (belonging to the school) of Isaiah. The term "the Holy One of Israel" met thirteen times in the first part of the book (Isa. 1:4; 17:7) occurs eleven times in the second section (e.g., Isa. 45:11; 55:5; 60:9) but only six times in the rest of the O.T.

In the Days of These Kings

The prophet Isaiah's threats of impending destruction and exile came to tragic reality in the fall of Samaria and in the exile of its people by Sargon in 722-721 B.C.—an event related both in the Old Testament (2 Kings 17) and in Sargon's records. Judah, taking no heed, continued its sinful way for slightly more than another century until she was dismembered in stages by Nebuchadnezzar. Daniel and his companions were carried off in 606 B.C. (Dan. 1:1). Jehoiachin and the noble class, following a capitulation to the Babylonians, were carried off in 597 B.C. This catastrophe is described both in the Old Testament (2 Kings 24:10-16; 2 Chron. 36:9-10) and in Nebuchadnezzar's annals. Jeremiah's prophetic career centers in the events of these and the following years. Then the eleven years' reign of Zedekiah climaxed in a second Judean revolt which resulted in the destruction of Jerusalem and an additional exile (2 Kings 25; Jer. 52) in 586 B.C. Yet still other exiles were taken in 582 B.C., the twenty-third year of Nebuchadnezzar (Jer. 52:30), under circumstances which we do not know.

However, following the destruction of Jerusalem the Exile slowly ran its course as Jeremiah had predicted it would (Jer. 25:1-12; 29:10). Cyrus then rose to power over Persia and, in 539 B.C., captured Babylon. Unlike the Assyrians and Babylonians who had controlled subject peoples by exiling, Cyrus, as attested by his famous cylinder which is in the British Museum, while giving credit to Marduk (the god of Babylon) for his victories, allowed subject peoples to return to their lands and to rebuild their ancestral temples that in every place prayer might be offered for Cyrus and his son Cambyses.

In keeping with the decree of Cyrus, Zerubbabel led a group of about fifty thousand Jewish exiles back to rebuild the temple in Jerusalem in 536 B.C. (Ezra 1:1ff.). Despite opposition of the people of the land and undue delay, the temple was completed and dedicated in 516 B.C. Then fifty-nine years later in 457 B.C., Ezra returned to teach the law and to carry through reforms. Still thirteen years later in 444 B.C. (ninety-two years after Zerubbabel's return), Nehemiah returned to rebuild the walls of Jerusalem. Nehemiah returned to Persia in 432 B.C. but then came back to Jerusalem (Neh. 13:6) and carried out additional reforms.

It is against this history that the message of the second portion of Isaiah is to be seen. The theme might be called "The Exile and its place in God's plan for Israel."

The Only God

Opening with the theme of comfort, Isaiah declares that in the Exile Israel had suffered commensurate with God's purpose (Isa. 40:1ff.). Though Jerusalem is addressed, the city stands for the whole people. As the end of the Exile and the preparing of the way in the wilderness for the returnees with the Lord as shepherd (Isa. 40:10-11) is proclaimed, the prophet affirms that none can stand in God's way of accomplishing his purpose. Certainly puny man cannot withstand him, for man is only flesh (Isa. 40:6-8), but God's word is forever. The good news is to be announced to Zion. All the nations are nothing before God (Isa. 40:17)—

a drop from a bucket or as dust on scales. A word to the discouraged assures them of God's help (Isa. 40:27-31). The Lord gives power to those exhausted (Isa. 40:28-31). Israel is not to be discouraged (Isa. 41:14-16). The Lord prepares the way in the desert and supplies needs (Isa. 41:17-20; 43:19-21) to accomplish the return (Isa. 42:14-17).

The idols certainly cannot oppose the Lord, for he is the only God, and the idols have no existence. The prophet pours great scorn upon the idol-makers who carve their idol, cover it with gold or silver, fasten it down securely, and fall before it proclaiming that it is the god who made them (Isa. 40:18-20; 41:6ff.; 44:6ff.; 46:5-7). Isaiah challenges the idol worshipers to tell either what has been or what is to be (Isa. 41:21-24). Let the idols do either good or evil, for they can do nothing. They are mere delusions (Isa. 41:29). The Lord, on the other hand, has formed Israel, has predicted, and has accomplished what has happened. Only he who controls the future can tell what will be. The Lord had threatened the Exile and has brought it into reality. Now he promises a new thing, namely, the return from the Exile, and nothing will stand in the way of his purpose (Isa. 47:9; 48:3ff.).

The Exile had tested belief. Some, like the prophets, interpreted it as a punishment of Israel for sin; others, no doubt like the foreigners brought into Samaria (2 Kings 17:24ff.), were greatly tempted to adopt the gods of the area to which they were carried. With a great deal of skill Isaiah describes the frantic haste to load the images of Nebo and Bel (Babylonian deities) upon the backs of animals to carry them to security, probably in the face of an enemy invasion; or, if this is not the purpose of their being carried, it is in the procession of the New Year's day (Isa. 46). Either way, they are a load to be borne by their worshipers. In contrast with the idols' helplessness, the Lord has borne Israel from childhood to old age (Isa. 46:4). We have to grant the prophet that it makes all the difference in the world whether you are carrying your God or whether he is carrying you.

The one God is not to be compared with anything (Isa. 40:25). He has created the heavens and earth (Isa. 40:12ff.; 42:5; 45:18f.; 48:12-13). He creates light and darkness, and both weal and woe (Isa. 45:7; cf. Job 2:10; Amos 3:6; Rom. 1:20). It is he who has redeemed Israel and who will be with her to accomplish her return (Isa. 43:1ff.). Fire,

The Major Prophets

water, distance, and people cannot frustrate him. The return is greater than the exodus from Egypt (Isa. 43:14-21). God has swept away Israel's sin (Isa. 44:22). He is the only God (Isa. 44:6-8; 45:5). Man is no more to argue with God's ways of accomplishing his purpose than the clay is to argue with the potter over what the potter is making (Isa. 45:9-12). God declares the end from the beginning; he has purposed and he will do it (Isa. 46:10-13). It is his decree that Jerusalem shall be inhabited (Isa. 44:24-27).

This God is the redeeming God. He gives Egypt, Ethiopia, and Seba as a ransom for Israel (Isa. 43:3-4). He is the forgiving God who removes the record of sin as though sweeping away a cloud (Isa. 44:22). He alone blots out sins (Isa. 43:23-25). He is the carrying and saving God (Isa. 46:3-40). Man is a creation of that God who gives breath (*neshamah*; cf. Gen. 2:7; 7:22; Isa. 2:22; Job 26:4) and spirit (*ruach*; Isa. 42:5).

Cyrus and the Lord

As we have earlier seen, Isaiah proclaimed that the Assyrian was a tool in God's hand (Isa. 10:5ff.), and later Jeremiah proclaimed that Nebuchadnezzar was the Lord's servant to accomplish the captivity of his people (Jer. 25:9; 27:6; 43:10). Now God has raised up Cyrus to accomplish the return of his people from exile. God has stirred him up from the east and has given him victory at every hand (Isa. 41:2-4). He tramples on rulers as the potter tramples the clay (Isa. 41:25).

Cyrus is the Lord's shepherd (Isa. 44:28)—a title frequently used of Middle Eastern rulers—he is the Lord's anointed (cf. 1 Sam. 24:6f.) whose right hand the Lord has grasped (Isa. 45:1). Only here in the O.T. is the term "his anointed" applied to a foreigner or a foreign king. The Lord has called Cyrus's name though Cyrus is unaware of it (Isa. 45:4). It is most interesting that in his cylinder Cyrus gives Marduk credit for his rise to power. Marduk has searched through the nations for a man of his choosing, has pronounced the name of Cyrus, and has gone at his side like a friend. But for Isaiah, Cyrus has been aroused in righteousness by the Lord; he will build the Lord's city and will set the exiles free without price (Isa. 45:13). Likely Josephus' statement (*Ant.* 11.1.2 [5]) that Cyrus had read this material of Isaiah is no more than a conjecture. Isaiah calls Cyrus "a bird of prey from the east" (Isa. 46:10-11).

The Lord's Witnesses

The reason why the God of the universe should have a special people Israel is not only often raised by the modern mind but is also dealt with in the Bible. Deuteronomy informs us that the choice of Israel was neither because of Israel's numbers (Deut. 7:7; cf. Deut. 14:2) nor because of her righteousness (Deut. 9:4-6), but was because God loved her (cf. Deut. 4:37; 10:14-15), and he is keeping the oath he made with the patriarchs. Amos 3:2 presents Israel's place, not so much as a place of privilege, as a place of responsibility.

One of the significant contributions to religious thought of Isaiah is his declaration on this theme. As the worshipers of idols are the witnesses of the idols, so Israelites are the Lord's witnesses (Isa. 43:9-10; cf. Acts 1:8) who attest that he has predicted the Exile and has accomplished it; hence, they are witnesses that he is the only God (Isa. 45:18-19, 22-25).

Israel is also the Lord's servant (Isa. 41:8) who has the task of being a light to the nations (Isa. 42:6; 49:6). The clay has no right to challenge the potter (Isa. 45:9-10; cf. Rom. 9:20-21) nor does the child before birth question the parent (Isa. 45:10). So Israel cannot question the Lord's actions. God, knowing Israel's stubbornness, has tested her in the furnace of affliction (Isa. 48:1-11).

To a discouraged people the prophet gives assurance that the exile has been because of their sins, not due to a lack of power on the part of the Lord. There has only been a separation in the relationship with God (cf. Isa. 54:6-7; 62:4). Hosea had spoken of God as the husband and Israel as his wife. No divorce has taken place (Isa. 50) that would stand in the way of bringing Israel back. Jeremiah declares that God gave the northern kingdom a certificate of divorce (Jer. 3:8). There is no outstanding debt owed to creditors that could hinder (Isa. 50:1; cf. 2 Kings 4:1). God had not sold Israel into slavery. While a mother may forget her child, God cannot forget Israel. They are inscribed on the palms of his hands (Isa. 49:15-16).

The prophet depicts the fall of Babylon (Isa. 47:1ff.). He had spoken of its overthrow in Isa. 43:14-15. Personified as a fastidious lady, Babylon experiences the fate of a refugee. God's anger delivered his people into her hands; but she showed no mercy. Babylon, in her pride, considered that her successes came by her own power. She thought she would not be a widow or suffer loss of children; but both will come in one day. Her enchantments and sorceries will not help her. Her allies are no more protection than stubble is from a fire. None can save her.

The cup of God's wrath has been drunk (Isa. 51:17-23). Zion should rouse herself from her stupor. The Lord promises to take the cup of wrath from her hand and pass it to her tormentors who have trampled her.

Zion is called upon to put on her festive garments and to shake off the bonds of captivity (Isa. 52:1ff.). A deliverance comparable to the earlier one from Egypt awaits her (Isa. 52:3-6). The good news of deliverance has come (Isa. 52:7ff.). But this exodus is not in trepidation as was that from Egypt (cf. Exod. 12:11; Deut. 16:3; Isa. 52:11-12).

Isaiah compares Zion to a previously barren woman who now needs to enlarge her tent to care for her children (Isa. 49:20; 54:1-2). Though she has been for a moment forsaken, God has everlasting love for her (Isa. 54:6-8). As firm as the covenant with Noah following the flood, more enduring than the mountains, is the Lord's promise that he will no longer be angry (Isa. 54:9-10). No weapon against Zion shall prosper (Isa. 54:15-17).

A great invitation is given to those who are thirsty to come for that which money cannot buy (Isa. 55:1ff.) Acceptance must be made while there is yet opportunity. Repentance is necessary. God's word will accomplish its purpose as surely as the rain does in causing seed to germinate. A return must take place.

Salvation is for all. Those previously excluded from the community are invited—the foreigner and the eunuch (Isa. 56:3ff.). False worship under corrupt religious leaders is denounced (Isa. 56:9-57:13). The leaders of Israel are blind (Isa. 56:10-12).

The Problem of Delay

However, Isaiah also struggles with the problem of delay. In spite of Israel's zeal in religious observances, the promises of God are slow in coming to fruition. Idolatry is futile (Isa. 57:3ff.). Hezekiah had said there would be peace in his time (Isa. 39:8); had Israel obeyed the Lord's commandments, her peace would have been like a river (Isa. 48:18); but there is no peace to the wicked (Isa. 48:22; 57:21).

The people ask why they have fasted and God had taken no notice (cf. Lev. 16:29-30; Isa. 58:1ff.). Externals had been observed (cf. Matt. 6:16-18). The Lord replies that the true fast is that of aiding the oppressed (Isa. 58:6). If they honor the Sabbath, God will bless them (Isa. 56:1ff.; 58:13). Sabbath observance was a significant duty under the law (Exod. 20:8). There is no adequate reason for assuming that this passage deals with Sabbath observance at the end of days.

The failure of the promised deliverance to appear is not due to inability on the part of God. The sins of the people are responsible for the delay (Isa. 59:1ff.). An extended indictment is made. The prophet makes a confession of sin (Isa. 59:12-15). The Lord threatens action at once against evildoers. He is described in armor (Isa. 59:17) which influences Paul's description in Ephesians 6:14ff.. The Lord judges the wicked.

Zion is called on to rise and shine (Isa. 60:1ff.) A picture of the regathering of her people is given. Foreigners rebuild her walls. The Lord smote in wrath but has had mercy on her.

Jesus read Isa. 61:1-2a in the synagogue at Nazareth and declared it fulfilled in what the audience was hearing (Luke 4:17-21). The remainder of the chapter speaks of restoration.

The prophet refuses to be silent short of the vindication of Zion (Isa. 62:1ff.). Upon the walls of Zion he sets watchmen to remind the Lord continuously of his promise to redeem Zion (Isa. 62:6ff.). A command to prepare the highway is given. The city will be called "a city not forsaken" (cf. Isa. 62:4). The new names are Hephzibah (My delight is in her) and Beulah (Married). Judah will enjoy the products of her toil (Isa. 62:8-9). Her salvation is coming (Isa. 62:10-12).

Numerous prophetic passages deal with Edom's punishment (cf. Mal. 1:2-5). Isaiah had an oracle on Edom in chapter 34 (cf. Ps. 137:7). Isa. 63:1-6 presents the Lord as a warrior who has come from vengeance on Edom. The image is of one treading the winepress with clothes stained. The Lord alone, without helper, has crushed Edom. The treading of the winepress image is also found in the book of Joel 3:13, the Lamentations 1:15, and then is used in the book of Revelation (Rev. 14:19, 20; 19:15).

With great pathos the prophet pleads with the Lord to rend the heavens and to go into action. Confessing complete unworthiness (Isa. 64:6), he pleads for the Lord's sympathy. The Lord is the potter; the people are the clay (Isa. 64:8). The temple lies in ruins, the city is destroyed; how can the Lord restrain his pity (Isa. 64:10ff.)?

Though the Lord is ready to be sought, he deals with a rebellious people whose idolatry is described as odious (Isa. 65:1-7). Punishment is necessary, but not all are guilty (vv. 8-10). The guilty are destined for the sword; but the Lord's servants are destined for joy.

The Lord creates a new heaven and a new earth (Isa. 65:17-25) which is an image that influences Rev. 21:1-2. Paradise conditions are described.

The last chapter (Isa. 66) mentions the Lord whom no house on earth can contain and affirms the Lord's concern for the humble person. Animal sacrifice is not what he is seeking. Zion is described as a nursing mother. Zion bringing forth children is not in the position Hezekiah described himself to be in (cf. Isa. 37:3). She has no lack of strength. Prosperity is promised.

Questions for Discussion

1. How did the policies of Cyrus differ from those of his Assyrian and Babylonian predecessors?

2. How do the two sections of Isaiah differ from each other?

3. What was taking place in Jerusalem at the beginning of the sixth century B.C.?

4. What lapse of time separates Zerubbabel and Nehemiah?

5. How does Isaiah describe idols?

6. What is Isaiah's chief argument for God's power?

7. What has Isaiah to say about the unlikeness of God?

8. What role has the Lord for Cyrus?

9. Why did the Lord choose the nation of Israel?

10. How does Isaiah explain why God's promises to Israel have not been realized?

Chapter V

THE MESSIANIC HOPE IN ISAIAH'S PROPHECIES

Introduction

Isaiah's vision, (often considered his call to prophesy) narrated in chapter six, concludes:

> "And though a tenth remain in it, it will be burned again, like a terebinth or an oak, whose stump remains standing when it is felled." The holy seed is its stump.

This vision brings before us the calamity to be faced, the remnant to survive, and the messianic future to grow out of the remnant (Isa. 6:11-13). While some interpreters, insisting that much of the book is later than the time of Isaiah, have attempted to deny any element of hope in authentic oracles of Isaiah, the hope element of the book is too prominent to be denied.

The book of Isaiah and the book of Psalms are the two books of the Old Testament most quoted in the New Testament. Christians have in all periods found in these books elements congenial to their faith. In addition to those passages specifically appealed to and interpreted by New Testament writers, there are a number of other passages which are traditionally interpreted messianically.

Isaiah's contribution to this messianic material may be classified in two categories: (1) Material dealing with a messianic age but which has no mention of a personal Messiah; (2) Material in which the Messiah plays a role. In this lesson these sections of the two categories are not to be considered in a chronological sequence.

The Messianic Age

Like many of the prophets, Isaiah's expectations for the future include a survival of a remnant which expectation in its original setting speaks of those who survive the calamity (the Assyrian invasion) with which Isaiah threatens his contemporaries (Isa. 10:20-23). Paul appealed to this remnant expectation (Rom. 9:27-29) to explain why the masses of Jews had not accepted the gospel. The Lord had promised only a remnant. Paul and the other believing Jews belonged to that remnant which would be saved.

The expectation of Isaiah included the return from exile which is presented in figures of a new exodus compared in wonders to the earlier exodus led by Moses. One of the most striking sections in which this expectation is set forth contrasts the perpetual desolation of Edom (Isa. 34) with the way of return in the desert (Isa. 35). The phrases of this description seem echoed in Heb. 12:12 (cf. Isa. 35:3, 4). Otherwise, this passage is not interpreted in the New Testament. However, the term "The Way" used for the early church (Acts 9:2; 24:14) is doubtless an echo of this passage of Isaiah combined with Isa. 40:3ff.

The night of exile fell first on the tribal areas of Zebulun, Naphtali, and on across the Jordan whose people were carried off by Tiglathpileser III when he was brought in by Ahaz to save himself from Pekah and Rezin in 734 B.C. (2 Kings 15:29). To these tribes Isaiah sees the light of redemption first dawning (Isa. 9:1ff.). Matthew found here words to describe the impact made on Galilee by Jesus during his early preaching (Matt. 4:15-16).

The transformed land is another aspect of the prophet's vision. In a passage directly paralleled by an oracle of his contemporary, Micah (Mic. 4:1-3), Isaiah sees Zion becoming the religious center of the world and the whole resulting in peace (Isa. 2:1ff.). Though this passage is not appealed to or interpreted in the New Testament, as early as the time of Justin Martyr (*Apol.* 1.39) and Irenaeus (*Adv. Haer.* 4.34.4) it was interpreted as predicting the gospel age. This passage has often been used in modern times in an argument to establish the date of the origin of the church. A sermon of five points centers around the key phrases: (1) The last days; (2) The Lord's House; (3) Established on the top of the mountains; (4) All nations flowing unto it; (5) The Word of the Lord going forth from Jerusalem. In this interpretation the peace envisioned becomes figurative and finds its fulfillment in the peace brought by Christ (Luke 2:14; John 14:27) as he broke down the middle wall of partition (Eph. 2:11-18). We shall return to the vision of peace later. Dogmatism about the interpretation of a passage not used in the N.T. is inappropriate.

It may be of interest to the student to be reminded that, with "law" (*torah*) understood in its wider meaning as "instruction," in Israel today "the law going forth from Zion" is a very frequently used phrase to describe Israel's part in the training of developing nations. It is difficult, however, to see in this action any real connection with Isaiah's intent.

The Messiah

The title "Messiah" (Gk.: *Christos*) arose from the practice of initiating a king into office by anointing with oil (2 Sam. 2:4; 2 Kings 11:12). The king was then known as the "Lord's anointed" (1 Sam. 24:10; 2 Sam. 19:21). However, as a technical designation "anointed" for a coming figure occurs only in Ps. 2:2 (quoted in Acts 4:25-26) and in Dan. 9:25 in the O.T.

The Virgin's Child

We have already in lesson two studied the sign promised Ahaz (Isa. 7:14) at the time of the Syro-Ephraimitic war. Matthew explained that this passage predicted the virgin birth (Matt. 1:23), and he set the stage for all later Christian treatment of the passage. Jewish exegesis has tended to see Hezekiah as the child spoken of by Isaiah. Strict chronology, however, would make it likely that Hezekiah had already been born before 734 B.C.; but the rabbis operated on the principle that there is no chronology in Scripture; hence, they were not bothered about Hezekiah's probable age at this time.

Immanuel

The name "Immanuel" (God with us) given to the child (Isa. 7:14; 8:8; cf. 8:10) is a further contact with New Testament thought. This element is also used by Matthew (Matt. 1:23) to explain the incarnation. A seal found in Jerusalem with the name `*Imanuyahweh* (The Lord is with us), as well as similar names occurring in the Elephantine Papyri, make it likely that a mother could have given her child such a name in Isaiah's time. If so, then Matthew is using this material in a typical way as he does "Out of Egypt have I called my Son." and "Rachel weeping for her children."

The Prince of Peace

A further item, not appealed to in the New Testament, is to be seen in the child spoken of in Isa. 9:6, 7. The government is to be upon his shoulder. He is to have four titles none of which are applied to Christ in the N.T.: (1) Wonderful Counselor, (2) Mighty God (cf. Isa. 10:21), (3) Everlasting Father, and (4) Prince of Peace. The KJV, by an unfortunate use of a comma between the two phrases of the first item (a punctuation further perpetuated by Handel's *Messiah*), made five titles of these words.

Since at least as early as the time of Irenaeus (*Adv. Haer.* 3:19.2-3, 21.1, 3; 4:32.11) this passage has been repeatedly applied to Jesus and used in an argument to establish his divinity. However, it is also interesting to notice that the first phrase in the Septuagint version became "Angel of mighty counsel," and it is this Septuagint phrase which seems most frequently commented on in early writers. In it was seen the work of Jesus as the revealer of God's will (Novatian, *On the Trinity* 18).

It would seem that the early rabbis, like early Christians, granted that this passage of Isaiah is messianic. However, in the Middle Ages there was an anti-Christian reaction which drove Rashi and those Jewish commentators who came after him to affirm that the passage deals with Hezekiah whose righteousness is contrasted with that of his predecessor Ahaz. In this interpretation, Hezekiah becomes the "Prince of Peace," and he is called that by the Wonderful Counselor, Mighty God, and Everlasting Father. In other words, in this exegesis the last three titles are considered descriptive of the speaker rather than of Hezekiah. The interpretation also involves a variant understanding of the phrase "and he will call" with that verb being taken as active voice singular rather than as the passive ("he will be called") which it was read in the Septuagint, and thereby by early Christians. The Hebrew consonants, but not the vowels, would be the same in either case. The traditional synagogue reading which the Masoretic text preserves is active voice. This represents a departure from the earlier Jewish interpretation in which the four titles were those of the child while at the same time there was a difference of opinion over whether the Messiah or Hezekiah was intended.

The Shoot of Jesse

The expectation of the rise of an ideal descendant of David ultimately goes back to 2 Samuel 7 where God, through the mouth of the prophet Nathan, promises to build David a house raising up one to sit upon his throne. This promise to David forms God's covenant with David alluded to in some Psalms (Ps. 89:[36]37]35-36; 132:11, 17) and is the start of the "Son of David" hope. Among the prophets it will be recalled that Amos had earlier pointed to the rebuilding of the dilapidated tent of David (Amos 9:11-12). Isa. 16:5 speaks of a throne in the tent of David and of a ruler on it.

In Isa. 11 the survival of the Davidic house is to be contrasted with the cutting of the trees brought by the Assyrian invasion seen in Isa. 10:19, 33, 34. A shoot (*choter*) paralleled to branch (*netser*) will grow up from the root (*sharash*) of Jesse (Isa. 11:1). Jeremiah speaks of a righteous branch (*tsemach*) of David (Jer. 23:5; 33:15), and Zechariah of the man whose name is the branch (Zech. 3:8). It has been tentatively suggested by some that the passage of Isaiah is the passage in the back of Matthew's mind when (in an otherwise unidentified citation) he says: "He shall be called a Nazarene" (Matt. 2:23). There can be no certainty in such matters. Paul appealed to this passage of Isaiah in Rom. 15:12 as a part of his argument of the inclusion of Gentiles in God's grace. It also lies back of "Root of David" of Rev. 5:5; 22:16.

This descendant of David is to be characterized by seven spirits all of which except the first are paired together: (1) The Spirit of the Lord; (2) the spirit of wisdom and understanding; (3) the spirit of counsel and might; (4) the spirit of knowledge and fear of the Lord. The writer seems to combine in this person the traits earlier manifested by David and Solomon. Righteous judgment is the characteristic of his activities. And a condition of peace, described in obviously figurative terms (vv. 6-9), is the result. The outcome of all is an earth full of the knowledge of the Lord as waters cover the sea. The degree to which these visions are to be understood literally is one of the most crucial issues between the millennial and non-millennial type of thinking, as well as between Jewish and Christian exegesis.

Jack P. Lewis

The Holder of the Key of David (Isa. 22:22)

Isaiah threatens the removal of Shebna from his position as "over the house," but he promises to Eliakim that position which Eliakim later occupied (Isa. 36:3; 37:2). Authority is promised him:

> I will place on his shoulder the key of the house
> of David; he shall open and none shall shut; he shall
> shut and none shall open (Isa. 22:22).

The key of David is not otherwise mentioned in the O.T., but the writer of the Apocalypse picks up this passage. To the church in Philadelphia it is said,

> The words of the holy one, the true one, who has
> the key of David, who opens and no one shall shut,
> who shuts and no one opens (Rev. 3:7).

The Messiah has the authority to admit or exclude people from the kingdom.

The Stone Laid in Zion

While the Judean politicians scoff at the prophet's advice, Isaiah calls their plans for alliance with Egypt a "covenant with death" (Isa. 28:15, 18). Faith in God is what gives Hezekiah and Judah a future. Isaiah reminds them that God is laying a cornerstone for the building (Isa. 28:16). By connecting this passage with Ps. 118:22 its messianic connection is to be seen. The concept was used by Jesus at the close of his parable of the wicked tenants (Matt. 21:42). Paul uses it when he relates how the unbelieving took offense at the Messiah (Rom. 9:33; 10:11). A more direct appeal is to be seen in 1 Pet. 2:6-8 where the passages from Psalms and Isaiah are contrasted. Jesus is known as the chief cornerstone (Eph. 2:20).

The King Who Reigns in Righteousness

Yet another of Isaiah's pictures is of the king who reigns in righteousness (Isa. 32:1-8). It is a picture of righteous government, of open understanding, and of the treating of each one in keeping with his true character. The contrasts between the fool and the wise man are obvious in the presentation.

The Servant of the Lord

Following a pattern set by Bernhard Duhm, it has been customary in the study of the second section of Isaiah to speak of "Servant Songs." Duhm envisioned four such sections (Isa. 42:1-4; 49:1-6; 50:4-9; 52:13-53:12) as having had independent existence before they were incorporated into their present setting. Other scholars have not always agreed with Duhm on the number and extent of these sections, but they have used his terminology.

The identity of the servant spoken of is one of the most disputed points in Isaiah study. While it is beyond dispute that in some sections the servant is identified with Israel (Isa 41:8, 9; 43:10; 44:1-2; 45:4; 49:3; etc.), when one comes to Isa. 53 the statements made about the innocent, uncomplaining sufferer who bears the sins of others do not seem rightly to characterize Israel's character, position, or attitude.

In general, however, Jewish scholars have favored a collective interpretation which makes Israel the servant. They then debate whether the suffering spoken of is past or is continuous. First century Judaism had no tradition of a suffering Messiah (cf. John 12:34). The earliest Jewish interpretation now known may be seen in the *Targum to Isaiah* where by paraphrase all the suffering is transferred to Israel's enemies. One of the most recent and most thoroughgoing Jewish interpretations is that of Harry Orlinsky.

On the opposite side of the question, Christians have tended to an individual interpretation but have differed widely over the nominees. Fifteen different Old Testament figures have at some time been suggested; but since no man can claim innocence or can expect that his death will make many righteous, none of these prove convincing. For these reasons it seems that only the Messiah can be envisioned.

In this section, the nations express surprise that things have turned out so differently from that which was expected. None could have understood had it been told them. One of no particular beauty has been despised and rejected of men, yet his mistreatment has a far different significance than was expected. While the nations thought of him as being smitten by God, it was really "for our transgressions that he was bruised." The speakers confess that though they had wandered like sheep, he as the uncomplaining victim was smitten "for the transgres-

Jack P. Lewis   **51**

sion of my people." "The Lord has laid on him the iniquity of us all." He is made an offering for sin; by his knowledge he will make many righteous. He was numbered with the transgressors; yet he bore the sins of many and made intercession for the transgressors.

This section of Isaiah has had a major impact upon the New Testament. In early Christian preaching Jesus was the servant (*pais*; the Greek rendering of '*ebhedh*) of the Lord (Acts 3:13; 4:27, 30). Philip preached Jesus to the Ethiopian beginning at this passage (Acts 8:35). In the Gospel of Matthew, Jesus' healing ministry is explained, "he took our infirmities and bore our diseases" (Matt. 8:17; cf. Isa. 53:4). Circumstances of Jesus' death are explained in the Gospel of Luke: "He was numbered with the transgressors" (Luke 22:37; cf. Isa. 53:12). Isa. 53 forms a focal point of the explanation of the significance of the death of Jesus in the first Epistle of Peter (2:22-25; cf. Isa. 53:5-6, 9, 12). There are also many other passing allusions to this section scattered through the New Testament. Christian interpretation has seen parallels to which special attention is not called in the N.T.: the silent sufferer (Isa. 53:7; Mark 15:5; Matt. 27:14), Jesus' prayer on the cross has been seen as "he made intercession for the transgressors" (Isa. 53:12; Luke 23:34), and he made his grave with the rich (Isa. 53:9; Luke 23:53).

Good Tidings to the Poor (Isa. 61:1ff.)

An unnamed speaker insists that possessing the Spirit of God and his anointing, it is his task to proclaim liberty to the captives; to proclaim the acceptable year of the Lord's favor. Jesus in the synagogue at Nazareth read this passage and insisted that it was fulfilled (Luke 4:18-19; cf. 7:22; Matt. 11:5).

Questions for Discussion

1. What two sorts of Messianic material does one find in the book of Isaiah?

2. What aspects of Isaiah's message are found in his "call vision"?

3. What role does the remnant play?

4. What is the history of interpretation of Isaiah 2:1-4?

5. To what family, and how, does Isaiah attach the Messianic hope?

6. What interpretations have been given to the Servant of the Lord?

7. Is a distinction to be made between material applied in the N.T. and interpretations that are only traditional?

8. What are Isaiah's pictures of the Messianic age?

9. What are the chief motifs in Isaiah's presentation of the Messiah?

10. How has Bernhard Duhm influenced study of the Servant in Isaiah?

Chapter VI

JEREMIAH

The Times of the Prophet

Almost a hundred years separate the main events of the career of Isaiah from those of Jeremiah. In 701 B.C. Sennacherib, having lost his army in the stroke from the Lord, withdrew from Jerusalem. Twenty years later he was murdered by his sons, and Esarhaddon, another son, came to the throne in Nineveh (Isa. 37:36-38; 2 Kings 19:36-37). During the seventy years from this point before the fall of Nineveh in 612 B.C., Assyria continued its expansion, and Egypt was conquered, in 667 B.C. by Ashurbanipal, the last major Assyrian king. In the late seventh century Assyria and Egypt who previously had been rivals became allies against the rising tide of Babylon with Egypt being an Assyrian vassal.

In Judah, Manasseh succeeded Hezekiah, submitted to Assyrian lordship, and brought back into Judah items from Assyrian religion. He refortified Jerusalem (2 Chron. 33:14). Despite Manasseh's fifty-five year reign (longer than any other Judean king), the writer of the book of Kings, because of Manasseh's filling Jerusalem with idolatry and with the innocent blood which was shed, considers him the worst of the Judean kings (2 Kings 21:1ff.; 2 Chron. 33:9; cf. Jer. 15:4). During his reign the Lord's decree of the destruction of Judah was announced.

Jeremiah, the son of Hilkiah, one of the priests of Anathoth which is a village slightly to the north of Jerusalem, prophesied chiefly from the thirteenth year of Josiah (626 B.C.) until the eleventh year of Zedekiah (586 B.C.), the year which saw the fall of Jerusalem to the Babylonians (Jer. 1:1-3). Jeremiah's final oracle, however, was uttered in Egypt after he had been taken there by his compatriots who feared reprisals from Nebuchadnezzar over the murder of Gedaliah, the Babylonian governor, by Ishmael (Jer. 40-44). The major events occurring in these more than forty years are surveyed in 2 Kings 22:3-25:26 and 2 Chron. 34:1-36:21. However, Jeremiah is only mentioned in them in connection with a no longer extant lament over Josiah (2 Chron. 35:25), in the statement that Zedekiah did not humble himself before Jeremiah the prophet (2 Chron. 36:12), and that the exile fulfilled Jeremiah's prediction of seventy years (2 Chron. 36:21-22).

Jeremiah's years were years in which there was a catastrophic realignment of international powers in the Middle East. Ashurbanipal, the last significant Assyrian king, died in 627 B.C. Josiah promptly carried through his reform in Judah in 622 B.C., exterminating remnants of the Assyrian cult (2 Kings 22-23) from Judah. The writer of the book of Kings does not point out the political implications of the reform. Onslaughts on Nineveh had begun to be made by the Babylonians as early as 626 B.C. Finally the city fell under the combined attack of the Scythians, Medes, and Babylonians in 612 B.C.— an event celebrated by the oracles of the prophets Nahum and Zephaniah. The remnant of the Assyrians fled westward and established themselves at Haran only to be attacked there by the Babylonians.

In 609 B.C. Josiah (who is praised by Jeremiah [Jer. 22:15-16]) lost his life vainly attempting to block the way of Neco as Neco went up from Egypt to aid Assyria in its final struggle with Babylon (2 Chron. 35:20-25). Jeremiah composed a lament over Josiah which is no longer extant. His son Jehoahaz (Shallum) replaced him for three months but was then taken to Egypt by Neco (Jer. 22:11-12). However, shortly thereafter a confrontation between Nebuchadnezzar and Pharaoh Neco at Carchemish in 605 B.C. (a battle recorded in the *Babylonian Chronicle*) ended disastrously for the Egyptians.

After experiencing a very brief period of domination by Egypt, Judah passed into the Babylonian sphere. In rapid order Jehoiakim, Jehoiachin, and Zedekiah occupied the throne of Judah. Nebuchadnezzar exiled portions of the people such as Daniel and his companions (Dan. 1:1-4) in 606 B.C. A few years later Jehoiakim was in revolt and Nebuchadnezzar again came west. However, before the siege proceeded far, Jehoiakim died and was replaced by his son Jehoiachin. After only three months' reign, Jehoiachin capitulated, and he along with the leading classes (including Ezekiel who later became a prophet) was taken

The Major Prophets

into exile. Jeremiah promises their return from exile (Jer. 24:6-7). The records of Nebuchadnezzar tell of his campaign and establish March 15-16, 597, as the date of Jerusalem's fall.

Mattaniah (Zedekiah) was next placed on the throne of Judah with an oath of allegiance to Babylon (2 Chron. 36:12-13), but, Zedekiah, unwilling to listen to Jeremiah, after eleven years was also drawn into revolt. This time in 586 B.C., Jerusalem was captured after a siege of eighteen months, the temple was destroyed, and the leading people exiled. After the debacle, Jeremiah, given a choice by the Babylonians, elected to remain behind with those left in Jerusalem. After a brief period of time, Gedaliah, who was appointed governor by the Babylonians, along with the Chaldean soldiers who were with him, was murdered by Ishmael. The people, fearing reprisals by the Babylonians, ignoring Jeremiah's advice, then fled to Egypt taking the prophet and Baruch with them. There Jeremiah continued his warnings against their idolatry, but we abruptly lose sight of him without knowledge of his ultimate fate. The writers of Kings and Chronicles follow the Babylonian exiles not the Egyptian refugees.

The Call of the Prophet

More is known about Jeremiah than is known about any other of the writing prophets. More is known about him and David than about any other O.T. personality. The priest Abiathar had been banished to Anathoth by Solomon when Abiathar had supported Adonijah (1 Kings 2:26-27). Jeremiah possibly was descended from Abiathar.

In calling Jeremiah to his task in 626, the 13th year of Josiah, God affirmed to the prophet that he had been appointed before he was born to be a prophet to the nations. To the prophet's protest (as Moses protested [Exod. 4:10-13]) that he was only a youth, the Lord promised that he would deliver him from opposition from all sources. The Lord touched Jeremiah's mouth and put his words in his mouth. As a prophet, Jeremiah was to pluck up and break down, destroy and overthrow, but also to build and plant (Jer. 1:5-10). Clearly his mission was both destructive and constructive. It is usually conjectured without specific evidence that Jeremiah may have been about age 20 when called.

To the Lord's query concerning what he saw (*ra'ah*), Jeremiah replied that he saw a rod of an almond (a *shaqed*). In a pun, the Lord replied that he was watching (*shoqed*) over his word to perform it (Jer. 1:11-12). The import is that the long delay had not nullified the Lord's threats against Jerusalem.

In a second vision the prophet saw a boiling pot facing from the north. He was informed that evil was about to break out of the north (cf. Jer. 4:13-16; 6:1, 22; 10:22; 13:20; 25:9). One of the significant questions in the interpretation of the book of Jeremiah has been that of the identity of the enemy out of the north. While some older scholars favored the Scythians (cf. Herodotus *Histories* 104) which danger never actually materialized as far as Judah is concerned, it now seems more likely that it was the Babylonians who already in 626 B.C. were making trouble for the Assyrians. The Scythians did not use chariots or siege engines (cf. Jer. 4:13; 5:15-17; 6:1-6). While Babylon is actually east of Jerusalem, an army in ancient times did not cross the desert; nor were sea landings made; hence, any invasion of Palestine not from Egypt must come from the north. In the face of the idolatry of his people and the arising danger, Jeremiah was to be a fortified city, an iron pillar, a bronze wall. He was to be one man against the nation. However, despite the opposition Jeremiah faced, the Lord promised that he would be with him and that he would prevail.

The Confessions

Jeremiah was apparently a man who enjoyed the company of people and who would have preferred to have their good will. However, the task given him by the Lord brought great conflict within his personality. As a man of strife and contention to the whole land (Jer. 15:10), he was torn between what he would have preferred to do and his sense of duty to the Lord. He gives utterance to these feelings repeatedly, and, following the title of the well-known book by Augustine (*The Confessions*), these sections (10:23-24; 15:10-21; 16:1-13; 17:9-10, 14-18; 18:18-23; 20:7-12, 14-18) have come popularly to be known as "Jeremiah's Confessions." It is debated among scholars whether these represent periods of despondency through which the prophet went throughout his entire career or whether they were a temporary phase out of which he emerged triumphant after the early days of his career. One view is that they date in the last part of Jehoiakim's reign. The

The Major Prophets

Lord answers three of the complaints (Jer. 11:18-23; 12:5-6; 15:19-21).

The Lord forbade that Jeremiah marry and beget children, or that he go to feasts, to weddings, or to funerals (Jer. 16:1-9) that he might be a walking lesson illustrating the fate to befall Jerusalem. He was forbidden that he should even pray in behalf of his people (Jer. 11:14; 14:11). In his misery, Jeremiah wished that he might weep day and night for the slain; he wished that he had a lodge in the wilderness where he could get away from it all (Jer. 9:1-3). In Jer. 10:23-24, the prophet confesses that he knows that the way of man is not in himself, and he requests correction only in just measure.

When Jeremiah heard that the men of Anathoth, his own townsmen, were plotting his death, he insisted that he was a lamb being led to the slaughter (Jer. 11:18ff.). He questions the justice of God which lets the wicked prosper (Jer. 12:1ff.). Rather than his receiving sympathy from the Lord, the Lord, using comparisons, replies to him in substance, "If you are troubled now, what will you do when the real difficulties arise?" (Jer. 12:5-6).

Jeremiah in his distress lamented that he had ever been born (Jer. 15:10; 20:14-18). The delay of the accomplishment of the threats he made caused him to be the laughing stock of his contemporaries. He complained about his loneliness (Jer. 15:17). He accused the Lord of being to him like a deceitful brook (Jer. 15:18); that is, like one that dries up. The Lord's reply is a call to repentance, and a challenge to distinguish between his own feelings and that which he has been commissioned to say. Should he do so, though fought against, he would prevail for the Lord would be with him (Jer. 15:19-21).

Following Jeremiah's being beaten and being put in stocks by Pashur the priest, the prophet accuses the Lord of having seduced him into being a prophet. The task has brought only reproach upon him. Yet when he vows that he will speak no more, he finds a burning fire in his bones which he cannot contain (Jer. 20:7-9). He curses the day that he was ever born and curses the man who brought the news of his birth. He cries, "Why did I come forth from the womb to see toil and sorrow and spend my days in shame?" (Jer. 20:14-18).

Oracles in the time of Josiah

Jeremiah's book of fifty-two chapters, represented by six manuscript fragments in the Qumran find (2QJer, 4QJer^a, 4QJer^b, 4QJer^c, 4QJer^d, 4QJer^e), occupies more space than any book in Scripture other than Psalms. Some portions of the book are narrated in first person and some in third person. Within the book the various oracles are arranged in a topical rather than in a chronological order. Some are dated enabling us to connect them with the crisis in which they were spoken; others can only be so related by conjecture. Chapters 1:1 and 3:6-25 are specifically dated in the reign of Josiah; but it is likely that all of chapters 1-6 form a unit from that time.

The sins of Judah as seen by Jeremiah are her idolatry, adultery, injustice, greed, deceit, and treachery. Over these sins the Lord states his legal case (*ribh*) through his prophet against Judah (called Israel since the northern kingdom was no more). Jeremiah sees the wilderness period as the honeymoon time of Israel's relations to God; but now that she has come into a good land she has turned to the worship of Baal (Jer. 2:1-9). She is God's own possession, but her present pathetic state has come about through her apostasy. Jeremiah argues that Israel's behavior is unnatural. No other nation has changed its gods even though they were no gods; but Israel has forsaken the fountain of living water in favor of a leaky cistern that can hold no water (Jer. 2:11-19).

In a series of figures the prophet depicts the depth and unnaturalness of Israel's sin. She is as an untamed calf who breaks its yoke (Jer. 2:20), as a harlot seeking illicit lovers (vv. 20b, 25), as a degenerate vineyard (v. 21; cf. Isa. 5:1ff.), as a dirty person whom soap will not cleanse (v. 22), as a young camel or wild donkey in heat (vv. 23, 24), as a thief caught red-handed (v. 26). Like the Ethiopian's skin or the leopard's spots (Jer. 13:23), Israel's sin is deeply ingrained; she refuses correction (Jer. 2:30). Though a girl cannot forget her jewelry, Israel has forgotten God (v. 32). Doing evil has become a skill (Jer. 4:22). The snow does not leave Mt. Hermon, but God's people forget him (Jer. 18:14-15).

Hauntingly the prophet uses the word "return" (*shubh*) and its derivatives (3:1, 7, 10, 12, 14, 22; 4:1). *Shubh* is the Hebrew word for repentance. As the divorced woman who has remarried may not return to her first husband (cf. Deut. 24:1-4), so Israel stained with the Canaanite cult cannot return to God. She is a shameless harlot (Jer. 3:1-5). Judah is even more sinful than Israel (who had now been in exile for a hundred years) for she refused to learn from Israel's sin and fate (Jer. 3:6-11). The Lord had divorced Israel (Jer. 3:8). Yet despite these things, the prophet issues a call to return to God (Jer. 3:12-14a). Should such a return take place, then a meager return from exile of a united people—one from a city and two from a family—is envisioned. The return is considered more marvelous than the Exodus from Egypt (Jer. 3:15-20). Both halves of the nation are involved (Jer. 3:18). In graphic terms the prophet describes Israel's hypothetical repentance (Jer. 3:21ff.). Returning to the Lord is needed. Fallow ground needs to be broken up (cf. Hos. 10:12) and hearts need to be circumcised (Jer. 4:1-4).

The prophet seems to have searched Jerusalem in vain for a righteous man (Jer. 5:1-3; cf. Gen. 18:22-32; Ezek. 22:30). When he thought depravity characterized only the poor, Jeremiah found the great to be equally guilty (Jer. 5:4-5). In their adultery he compared them to well-fed lusty stallions neighing after their neighbor's wife (Jer. 5:7-8). They refused to believe the Lord would bring evil upon them (Jer. 5:10-13; cf. Zeph. 1:12). Like the sea that perpetually dashes against a barrier it cannot pass, so God's people rebel against him (Jer. 5:20-25). The wicked entrap men as fowlers catch birds (Jer. 5:26-29). The prophets prophesy falsely and the people love it (Jer. 5:30-31).

God is about to pour out wrath on all strata of society. From the least to the greatest they are unjust. Priest and prophet say "'Peace, peace' when there is no peace" (Jer. 6:13-14; cf. 8:11). The word of the Lord is an object of scorn (Jer. 6:10). Some denied that they had sinned (Jer. 2:23; 16:10); others blamed their ancestors (Jer. 31:29). Jeremiah accuses them of being worse than their fathers (Jer. 16:12). When called to repent, they refuse the old paths; when sentinels warned, they did not heed (Jer. 6:16ff.). Jeremiah insists that sacrifice cannot avail for them (Jer. 6:20ff.). Borrowing an image from the metal industry, the prophet is a tester of the people, but they refuse to be refined (Jer. 6:27-30).

In the light of their sins, the enemy from the north is about to break forth to besiege Jerusalem (cf. Jer. 4:5ff.). It is a cruel nation from afar

(Jer. 6:22-26).

Other figures for the unnaturalness of sin are seen in the prophet's assertion that if a man falls down he gets up again; if he gets off the road, he turns back to it; but Israel is bent on backsliding (Jer. 8:4f.). The birds are controlled in their migration by a law of God (Jer. 8:7), but Judah does not obey the Law.

Jeremiah found no pleasure in the message he proclaimed. For the people he wept bitterly (Jer. 13:17). He did not desire the day of disaster (Jer. 17:16). He pled with the Lord (Jer. 4:10); he spoke good of the people (Jer. 18:20). Repeatedly he is told not to pray for them because they persist in sin (Jer. 7:16; 11:14; 14:11). The prophet cries that the harvest is past without salvation; though there is balm available, still healing does not take place (Jer. 8:19-22). The prophet can only give way to hopeless tears (Jer. 9:1ff.). He calls for the wailing women to come weep over the doomed city (Jer. 9:17ff.).

Since many of the sections of Jeremiah are undated it is only by conjecture that one can assign them to a particular time in his career. They are possible at any time from the start of his career to its end.

Scholars debate heatedly Jeremiah's attitude toward the reform of Josiah in 622 B.C., Josiah's eighteenth year The Book of Kings does not allude to Jeremiah at this period (2 Kings 22) or at any other time. When the book of the law was found in the rubbish of the temple, Huldah rather than Jeremiah was consulted to authenticate it. Nevertheless, some scholars have thought that they found evidence in Jeremiah's book that Jeremiah was very enthusiastic for the reform at first but later found that it failed in its purpose and that the priests of Jerusalem were using it to personal advantage; hence, he proceeded unhesitatingly to denounce its outcome. The case turns upon certain expressions in chapter 11:1-8. The word "covenant" (vv. 3, 6, 8) is conjecturally identified with Josiah's covenant (2 Kings 23:3). Furthermore, there is allusion in Jeremiah to certain matters found in Deuteronomy such as the marriage law (Jer. 3:1; cf. Deut. 24:1ff.). Then the release of male and female slaves (Jer. 34:8ff.) is thought to reflect the law about release of Hebrew slaves as stated in Deuteronomy 15:12f. However, the covenant spoken of in Jeremiah may be that made at Sinai and not that of Josiah at all. The other items in the case are striking only when one has previously concluded that the writing of Deuteronomy is at the time of the reform.

The case for Jeremiah's turning to denounce Josiah's reform is no more convincing than that of his advocacy for it. That it had been introduced in falsehood ("the false pen of the scribes has made it into a lie" [Jer. 8:8ff.]) is dependent upon M. de Wette's case for a pious fraud in the introduction of the book of Deuteronomy. De Wette argued that Deuteronomy had just been written and was intentionally passed off as the work of Moses. That Jeremiah's opposition to the reform is due to his attitude toward sacrifice presupposes the debatable proposition that he opposed sacrifice *per se*. It is quite possible to take his anti-sacrifice statements in a comparative way.

Out of it all, one may conclude that the case for Jeremiah's having failed twice as a prophet (once when the enemy from the north did not bother Judah and once over the reform of Josiah), and in chagrin his having gone into a thirteen year silence, is not established. Undated material in the book may fit the period of Josiah.

After Josiah's tragic death at Megiddo when Josiah vainly attempted to block Pharaoh Neco (cf. 2 Chron. 35:20-24), Jeremiah said of him that Josiah did justice and righteousness, that he judged the cause of the poor and needy (Jer. 22:15-16). The book of Chronicles informs us that Jeremiah uttered a lament for Josiah (2 Chron. 35:25) which is no longer extant.

Questions for Discussion

1. What are the visions that set Jeremiah on his career?

2. What is meant by the "Confessions of Jeremiah"?

3. What was Jeremiah's attitude toward prophesying?

4. What important events occurred during Jeremiah's career?

5. What are some of Jeremiah's images for the unnaturalness of sin?

6. What is Jeremiah's attitude toward various religious exercises?

7. Who is Jeremiah's enemy out of the north?

8. What is the Lord's response to Jeremiah's attitudes?

9. What is Jeremiah's evaluation of the people of Jerusalem?

10. What role does Jeremiah play in the narrative of the book of Kings?

Chapter VII

JEREMIAH, PART II

The Throne

Jeremiah, recognizing that Josiah had done justice and righteousness judging the cause of the poor and the needy, lamented his tragic death at Megiddo (cf. 2 Chron. 35:25). Following that tragedy and the deportation to Egypt of Jehoahaz, Josiah's son who had occupied the throne only three months (2 Kings 23:30-33; 2 Chron. 36:1-4), Jeremiah called for weeping over the exiled king whom he called Shallum whom Neco had carried off and who would not return (Jer. 22:10-12).

Jehoahaz was followed on the throne by Jehoiakim (Eliakim), another son of Josiah. The Egyptians apparently found Jehoiakim more satisfactory for their purpose than they did Jehoahaz. Josephus later said that Jehoiakim was "Neither reverent toward God nor kind to man" (*Ant.* 10.5.2 [83]).

The Temple At the beginning of Jehoiakim's reign (609 B.C.), Jeremiah appeared in the temple to denounce the false confidence which the presence of the temple inspired in the people (Jer. 7; 26). Jeremiah's temple sermon raised the basic question of what gives safety. Is it the temple and worship there or is it upright living? It was justice and not sacrifice which the Lord demanded. Jeremiah saw that the temple had become a den of robbers rather than a place of true worship (cf. Jer. 7:11; Mark 11:17). Jeremiah threatened that Jerusalem would be destroyed as Shiloh earlier had been (1 Sam. 4-6). The temple was no more a talisman now giving safety than the ark of the covenant had been in the time of Eli (1 Sam. 4:10-22). Observance of rites did not give security. The rite of circumcision in itself carried no more safety for Israel than it did for other circumcised peoples (Jer. 9:25-26). In one of the greatest of his statements, Jeremiah insists that true knowledge of God was really the essential thing which the Lord required (Jer. 9:23, 24). The Lord delights in steadfast love, justice, and righteousness.

When charged with treason for his statements threatening the temple, Jeremiah barely escaped when the princes and the people recalled that about a hundred years earlier Micah had threatened Jerusalem but had escaped when his threat brought Hezekiah to repentance, and the threatened calamity was averted (Jer. 26:16-19). Ahikam the son of Shaphan was a defender of Jeremiah (Jer. 26:24; cf. 2 Kings 22:12, 14; 25:22). In contrast to Jeremiah's fate, his contemporary, Uriah, had an entirely different fortune when after such a threat he fled to Egypt, was extradited, and was executed (Jer. 26:20-23).

Though Jeremiah denounced trust in the temple in the absence of moral behavior, he was far from being opposed to religious observances. He was commissioned to stand in the People's Gate and to call on the king, the people of Judah, and the inhabitants of Jerusalem to observe the sabbath properly. With proper observance of the sabbath, he promised there would be kings on the throne of David and people coming from all areas for temple rites. Refusal of observance would bring calamity (Jer. 17:19-27; 22:1ff.).

Like other prophets, Jeremiah insisted that under the conditions which existed the offering of incense and sacrifices was unacceptable (Jer. 6:20). He ironically suggests the obliteration of various sorts of sacrifice (Jer. 7:21).

Depravity

Jeremiah was banned from going to the temple (Jer. 36:5). By numerous homely figures the prophet pointed out the depth of depravity of his people. At the Lord's bidding he hid at the Euphrates a loincloth which he had worn, and later he returned to find it spoiled beyond using. As he explained his action, he made clear that in a like way, Judah, designed to be close to the person of the Lord, would be spoiled, for in its idolatry the people had become good for nothing (Jer. 13:1-11).

Jeremiah also said, "Every jar shall be filled with wine," a statement which appeared to his hearers as a superfluous statement. Its meaning was that the inhabitants of Jerusalem would be drunken and be destroyed (Jer. 13:12ff.). Exile awaited them (Jer. 13:23ff).

By especially graphic images the prophet described a drought they had experienced (Jer. 14:1ff.). The people were a people who loved to wander but whom the Lord would surely punish (Jer. 14:10ff.). Though the false prophets promised peace, God charged the prophet Jeremiah not to pray for the people (Jer. 14:11ff.). Should even Moses and Samuel (two great intercessors of the past) plead for them, it would go unheard. The sword, the dogs, the birds of the air, and the beasts of the earth were God's appointed agents of destruction (Jer. 15:1ff.). Jeremiah charged that Jerusalem habitually rejected the Lord. The Lord was tired of relenting; he would give her to the sword of the enemy (Jer. 15:6ff.).

Rather than Judah's sin being merely a thin veneer which could be removed to get down to the essential goodness, her sin is engraved on their hearts with an iron pen with a diamond point (Jer. 17:1ff.). Yet even such depravity is not completely irreversible. The prophet was commissioned to observe the potter take clay which had broken while being formed into a vessel and remold it into another vessel suitable to his will. So God can remold Judah. The threats and promises of God are conditional. Should a people turn to evil, promises of God will be revoked; should they repent, a threat previously made will be withdrawn (Jer. 18:1ff.). Surely here the prophet announced one of the most important considerations in interpreting the prophetic oracles. Such an oracle is conditional. It is not a decree that must be carried out as a decree of fate must be.

Meanwhile the outlook was not optimistic. The prophet was commissioned to take an earthen flask into the valley of Hinnom and to declare that the Lord was bringing evil upon Jerusalem because of its idolatry. He was to break the flask so that it could not be repaired. In that way he demonstrated that the coming damage to Jerusalem could not be repaired (Jer. 19:1ff.). Jeremiah's preaching brought him a beating at the hands of Pashhur the priest who was in charge of the temple. Jeremiah was placed in stocks, but when he was released, he threatened that Pashhur's friends would fall by the sword and that the priest himself would be carried into Babylon where he would die and be buried (Jer. 20:1ff.).

A Scroll

One of the most distinctive clashes between Jeremiah and King Jehoiakim came in Jehoiakim's fourth year when at the Lord's command Jeremiah dictated his oracles to Baruch who in turn read them to the people in the fifth year at a gathering in the temple, and then to the princes. They saw that the oracles reached the king. A Hebrew papyrus as old as Jeremiah has been found in the Wadi Murabba'at near the Dead Sea. Writing was well known in his time. The Lord's order at this point was not Jeremiah's first order to write (Jer. 30:1-2; cf. 51:60). After hearing a few pages read, the king hacked up the book and burned it. Jeremiah, however, redictated and added much more, declaring an approaching end to the dynasty of Jehoiakim (Jer. 36). The danger had not been averted by muzzling the prophet.

A bulla (clay with a stamp on it) belonging to Gemaryahu, son of Shaphan (presumably the person of this story) was found in the City of David excavations in 1982. Gemariah and two others supported Jeremiah (Jer. 36:25). There are also bullae of Baruch son of Neriah the scribe (cf. Jer. 36:4) and of Jerahmi'el the son of the king (cf. Jer. 36:26).

At this period Baruch gave way to an utterance of self-pity only to have his troubles compared with those of the Lord who was tearing down what he had built. For his service, Baruch was promised his survival in the calamity (Jer. 45:1ff.).

The Fourth Year

Jeremiah, following the battle of Carchemish in 605 B.C., celebrates the defeat of Egypt (Jer. 46:1-12). A number of Jeremiah's oracles are to be dated in the fourth year of Jehoiakim, that is, in 603/4 B.C. By this time, Jeremiah had been a prophet for about twenty-three years (Jer. 25:3). He announced that because of the refusal of Israel to obey and abandon its idolatry, the Lord was about to bring one called "Nebuchadnezzar my servant" (Jer. 25:9; 27:6; 43:10) against the land. Its desolation was to last for seventy years (Jer. 25:11; 29:10). It is as if Jeremiah were handing out a cup filled with the wine of God's wrath that the nations, including Judah, must drink even if they refuse to do so (Jer. 25:15ff.).

It may be at this time (though one cannot be certain) that Jeremiah's various oracles against the nations were spoken. As in the books of Isaiah, Amos, and Ezekiel, a more or less fixed group of nations are dealt with: Egypt, Philistia, Moab, Edom, Ammon, Damascus, Kedar, Hazor, and Elam (Jer. 46-49). Each must face the Lord's wrath. Babylon was being used by the Lord to punish Judah; but Babylon too must one day face the Lord's wrath.

Also sometime during the reign of Jehoiakim, Jeremiah had occasion to draw attention to the Rechabites who, in the face of the danger from Babylon, had moved from their nomadic life into the city of Jerusalem. When offered wine they refused to drink for they had been charged by their ancestor Jonadab ben Rechab (cf. 2 Kings 10:15) not to build houses, not to sow seed, and not to plant vineyards. Jeremiah draws a sharp contrast between their loyalty to the command of a man and Judah's disregard for the command of God, promising the Rechabites continuance before the Lord (Jer. 35:1ff.).

Jeremiah had found king Jehoiakim to be a vain, ruthless ruler who had carried out the building of his palace at the expense of his subjects. He reminded him that doing justice and righteousness was the condition of continuation of kings upon the throne of David; but failure to be righteous would end in destruction of the king's house (Jer. 22:1ff.). He contrasted Jehoiakim's extravagances and oppressions with the righteousness that earlier characterized Josiah's reign. And in one of his sternest oracles he promised that the king would be buried as a donkey is buried, dragged forth from the gates of Jerusalem (Jer. 22:13-19; cf. 36:20ff.).

Jehoiakim's policies brought the wrath of Nebuchadnezzar upon Jerusalem, but he, himself, did not live to see the tragic outcome. The circumstances of his death are unknown (cf. 2 Kings 24;6; 2 Chron. 36:5-8). His son, Jehoiachin, at age eighteen succeeded to the throne; but Jeremiah found Jehoiachin no more satisfactory as a ruler than had been his predecessor. He stated that though Jehoiachin (Coniah/ Jechoniah) were as close to the Lord as the signet on the Lord's hand (which he certainly was not), he still would be exiled and would die in captivity. He was a despised, broken vessel whose descendants would never prosper on the throne of Jerusalem (Jer. 22:24ff.). And so it was.

After only three months' reign, Jehoiachin capitulated to Nebuchadnezzar. Along with the artisans of the land, he was carried into captivity. The *Babylonian Chronicle* surveys the campaign of Nebuchadnezzar against Jerusalem and established the date of its fall as March 15/16, 597 B.C.

Zedekiah

Following the exile of Jehoiachin and the ten thousand most important members of the community, Nebuchadnezzar placed Mattaniah, a son of Josiah, on the throne with an oath of allegiance (2 Chron. 36:13), giving him the name Zedekiah. Zedekiah was only twenty-one years old (Jer. 52:1ff.). In the early days of Zedekiah's reign, Jeremiah spoke oracles of doom against Elam and Babylon (Jer. 49:34-51:64). The major concern of the prophet at this time, however, was the undue spirit of optimism which characterized his people. Those in Jerusalem felt that they had been spared the Exile because of their righteousness while those in exile were suffering for their sins. In reply Jeremiah described a vision of two baskets of figs, one good and one too rotten for use. In the interpretation of the vision, the good figs were the people already in exile while the bad figs were those left behind in Jerusalem who were soon to be made an object lesson to all the nations (Jer. 24:1ff.).

Early in Zedekiah's reign Zedekiah convoked an anti-Babylonian conference of neighboring countries (Edom, Moab, Ammon, Tyre, and Sidon) in Jerusalem. At the Lord's instigation, Jeremiah made himself a wooden yoke to wear as a symbol that all should submit to the yoke of Nebuchadnezzar. Zedekiah was advised to submit. Jeremiah exhorted the priests and people not to listen to those who said that the vessels already carried to Babylon would shortly be back. Such optimistic prophets, if they hoped to aid, should be interceding with the Lord that what yet remained in Jerusalem might not be carried to Babylon (Jer. 27:1ff.).

Clashing Prophets

However, one Hananiah of Gibeon said that the Exile would be over in two years and that Jeconiah would be back on the throne. Jeremiah could only express a wish that it might be so; but he reminded Hananiah that previous prophets had been prophets of doom speaking of war, famine, and pestilence. The prophet of weal is only to be believed after the good he promises is realized. Hananiah, however, in a symbolic act underscored his word by proceeding to break the yoke from Jeremiah's neck as a sign that the bondage to Nebuchadnezzar was shortly to be broken. Jeremiah had no immediate reply. After the passage of some time, Jeremiah was sent to say to Hananiah that an iron yoke had replaced the wooden one. For his false prophecy, Hananiah was to die that year; and in the seventh month of the same year he died (Jer. 28:1ff.).

Further evidence of Jeremiah's conflict with others claiming to be prophets but who were saying the opposite things from him is to be seen in his accusation that these prophets prophesy visions out of their own minds assuring the people that all will be well (Jer. 23:16-17). They had no commission from the Lord, but they ran anyway. They should be turning people from their evil way, but their prophecies are deceit out of their own heart. They borrow oracles from each other. In contrast to them, the one who has the Lord's word must speak it faithfully (Jer. 23:21-32). In what seems to be a play on the word *massa'* (burden) which is the technical term for a prophetic oracle but which also may mean "that which is lifted up," the prophet states that when one asks, "What is the burden (oracle) of the Lord?" he is to be told, "You are the burden (load) the Lord has to endure." Because the prophets have falsely spoken of the burden of the Lord, they will be lifted up and cast from the city (Jer. 23:33ff.)

Prophets in Babylon also were keeping the people agitated with false hopes of a brief exile and a speedy return to Jerusalem. By letter, Jeremiah advised the exiles to build houses, plant gardens, marry off their children and seek the welfare of the city where they were, for in its welfare they would find their own. The Exile was to last seventy years (Jer. 29:1-14). Jeremiah saw the future of the nation resting on those in exile. He insisted that those remaining behind in Jerusalem were doomed for their wickedness (Jer. 29:15-20). No hope was to be found there.

Furthermore, the prophets Ahab and Zedekiah, who were the trouble-makers in the midst of the Exile, would be slain by Nebuchadnezzar for their lies. They had even been guilty of adultery with their neighbors' wives (Jer. 29:21-23; cf. 23:14).

Shemaiah, another exile, went so far as to write Zephaniah the priest in Jerusalem urging him to curb Jeremiah's activities. He called Jeremiah a "madman" for his advice concerning appropriate action during the Exile. Jeremiah's reply is an oracle which threatens that none of Shemaiah's descendants would see the good the Lord proposed for his people (Jer. 29:24-32).

Babylonian Siege

In time, history repeated itself, and Zedekiah was drawn by the Judean politicians into revolt against Nebuchadnezzar. Vainly it was thought that the aid of Egypt could give Judah her independence from her overlord. The outcome was disastrous. Nebuchadnezzar came west to besiege Jerusalem, to take it, and to destroy the city.

During the siege, Jeremiah was at the height of his career. He announced that God was giving the city to Nebuchadnezzar; yet he promised that Zedekiah, though to be captured, would survive and die in peace (Jer. 34:1ff.). Already by this time Nebuchadnezzar had taken all the fortified cities except Lachish and Azekah (Jer. 34:6-7). Interestingly enough, in the excavations at Lachish twenty-one ostraca were found which seem to date at this period. They are in part correspondence from Judean military commanders in the Lachish region. On one, these very same two cities of which Jeremiah speaks are mentioned: "We are looking for the signals of Lachish for we cannot see those of Azekah," says the writer.

In what would seem to be a sort of deathbed repentance the Judeans freed their Hebrew slaves only shortly thereafter to break their covenant and take them back (Jer. 34:8-22). Perhaps the Babylonian siege had temporarily been lifted to deal with Egypt (Jer. 37:5). Playing on the word liberty, Jeremiah declares that since the Judeans have not kept the law which demanded giving liberty (cf. Lev. 25:39ff.; Deut. 15:12), they will have the liberty of being victims of the sword, famine, and pestilence. The one who breaks a covenant is to be treated as the sacrificial animal which is cut into pieces at the covenant-making ceremony (cf. Gen. 15:9-11, 17). Zedekiah and the princes are to be delivered to the king of Babylon.

As the war developed, Zedekiah at times sent to Jeremiah for advice. Perchance the Lord might perform a miracle and save him (as he had done for Hezekiah a century before?). Jeremiah assured him that quite to the contrary the Lord would defeat his efforts at war and that he would be delivered over to Nebuchadnezzar (Jer. 21:1-7). To the people, the prophet offered the way of life and death. Death faced those who stayed in Jerusalem, but life could be had by those who deserted to the Babylonians (Jer. 21:8ff.).

An approach of the Egyptian army to aid Jerusalem brought a momentary withdrawal of the Babylonians. It may be at this time that the taking back of the slaves spoken of above took place. Jeremiah, however, insisted that the Babylonians would be back. Should the Babylonians be defeated and be in such bad condition that there were only wounded men in the tents they would rise up and burn Jerusalem (Jer. 37:1-10).

During the interlude in the siege Jeremiah attempted to leave the city, perhaps to visit his hometown of Anathoth. Accused of intending to desert to the Babylonians, he was beaten and imprisoned in the house of Jonathan the secretary which house had been made into a prison. But at the instigation of the king he was removed to more comfortable quarters in the police guardhouse. Upon such occasions as the king asked for his advice, Jeremiah advised that the case was hopeless. Zedekiah would be delivered to the Babylonians (Jer. 37:16-21).

No people at war would tolerate the talk openly of a man like Jeremiah. With the renewal of the siege he was accused of "weakening the hands of the people" (the same phrase occurs in another context in the Lachish letters). The princes then let Jeremiah down into a cistern by ropes where he sank in the mire. However, Ebedmelech, an Ethiopian, with the knowledge of the king, raised him from the cistern (Jer. 38:1ff.). For his deed, Ebedmelech was promised survival of the calamity (Jer. 39:15-19). Jeremiah then was kept in the court of the guard.

To the king's queries about the fate in store for him, Jeremiah insisted that surrender was the only course of action. The king claimed he was afraid of those who had already deserted to the Babylonians. The prophet replied that he need not fear them, but refusal to surrender could only lead to the burning of the city (Jer. 38:14ff.). Jeremiah remained a semi-prisoner in the court of the guard until the fall of the city.

The Catastrophe

Jerusalem fell to Nebuchadnezzar the 9th of Ab (July) of 587/6 B.C. after a siege of eighteen months (Jer. 39:1-2; 2 Kings 25:8-21). Zedekiah and his court made a vain dash for safety, but they were caught in the plain of Jericho. Taken northward into the presence of Nebuchadnezzar at Riblah, Zedekiah saw his sons killed, and then he, himself, was blinded and taken to Babylon (Jer. 39:4-7) where he ultimately died in exile (Jer. 52:11). Ezekiel who was a prophet in the Exile had said Zedekiah would not see Babylon but would die there (Ezek. 12:13). The people of Judah, except for some of the poor, were taken by Nebuchadnezzar through Nebuzaradan, the captain of the guard, into exile (Jer. 39:9-10). However, special instructions were given by Nebuchadnezzar for the treatment of Jeremiah (Jer. 39:11-13). Given the option at Ramah of going to Babylon or of remaining behind, Jeremiah elected to remain with Gedaliah at Mizpah (Jer. 40:1-6). Gedaliah was the son of Ahikam who earlier had defended Jeremiah.

Gedaliah

Obviously despairing of controlling Judah through a Davidic prince, Nebuchadnezzar now appointed Gedaliah to be governor with his seat of government at Mizpah (thought to be the site of Tell en-Nashbeh eight miles north of Jerusalem). Gedaliah advised the people to settle down again, to gather their crops, and to serve Babylon. Refugees returned from neighboring areas to their homes. However, a certain Ishmael, son of Nethaniah, with the support of Baalis king of the Ammonites, murdered Gedaliah, the Chaldean soldiers with him, and some seventy others from Shechem, Shiloh, and Samaria who had come up to worship even after the temple had been destroyed (Jer. 40:13-41:17). It is thought that Gedaliah had governed from 586-582 B.C.

Faced now with the prospect of additional reprisals from Nebuchadnezzar for the murder of the governor, the people consulted Jeremiah about the advisability of flight to Egypt. Ten days later when the answer came to Jeremiah, he advised against their plan. Accusing him of being overly influenced in his answer by Baruch, they rejected his advice and carried him with them as they fled to Egypt (Jer. 42:1-43:7). Five years after the flight of these people to Egypt, another deportation for unknown causes completed the exiling of Judah (Jer.

The Major Prophets

52:30).

In Egypt, Jeremiah predicted an invasion of Egypt by Nebuchadnezzar (Jer. 43:8ff.), sternly denounced the idolatries of the Judeans, and threatened destruction both for them and Pharaoh Hophra under whose aegis they had sought protection (Jer. 44:1ff.). Nebuchadnezzar did attack Egypt in 562 B.C. (cf. Jer. 44:28; 46:13). It is here in Egypt that Jeremiah disappears from history. There is a legend that his people stoned him to death (Tertullian, *Scorpiace* viii; Jerome, *Adv. Jov.* II.37). Jewish tradition, however, has him escape from Egypt and accompanied by Baruch to go to Babylon where he died.

Questions for Discussion

1. What was Jeremiah's attitude toward king Johoiakim?

2. What gives safety according to Jeremiah?

3. What did Jeremiah see as the basic condition of the people of Jerusalem?

4. What did king Jehoiakim think of Jeremiah's prophesying?

5. How did Jeremiah see other prophets of his time?

6. How did Jeremiah see the obligation of the people of Jerusalem and of the people already in exile?

7. How did Jeremiah appear in the eyes of the people of Jerusalem?

8. What were Jerusalem's alternatives?

9. What conditions took Jeremiah to Egypt?

10. What is the nature of a prophecy as described by Jeremiah?

Chapter VIII

JEREMIAH, PART III

"Concerning the Nations" (Jer. 46-51)

Isaiah, Ezekiel, Amos, Nahum, Obadiah, and Zephaniah all have oracles concerning the nations. Jeremiah was called to be a prophet to the nations (Jer. 1:5). His oracles on the nations are placed in the Greek Bible following Jer. 25:13 in a different position and different order from their place and order in Hebrew which is followed by Latin and English.

Egypt. Jeremiah begins his oracles on the nations with words about Egypt and Pharaoh Neco's army at Carchemish for which he predicts defeat (Jer. 46:1ff.). He compares Egypt's efforts at expansion to the rising of the Nile (Jer. 46:7-8), but the battle is the Lord's sacrifice in the north country. Nebuchadnezzar is the implement by which Egypt is smitten. Pharaoh is the "Noisy one who lets the hour go by." Egypt's defeat spells the end of her dreams of world domination. Inhabitants of Egypt are destined for exile. Egypt is compared to a heifer annoyed by a gadfly, to one making the sound of a serpent sliding away, and to trees that are being cut. Egypt is to be delivered into the hands of Nebuchadnezzar. Nebuchadnezzar invaded Egypt in 568 B.C., but the outcome did not result in her becoming uninhabited. The chapter ends with a promise of return from exile for Jacob after punishment.

The Philistines. The Philistines have left their name on the land in the title "Palestine." Like Amos, Jeremiah identifies them as being from Caphtor (Jer. 47:4; Amos 9:7). The location of the Philistine cities Gaza, Ashkelon, Ashdod, and Ekron have been identified; the location of Gath remains unknown. Ashkelon (a site covering 150 acres) has yielded remains identified by the excavator with the Babylonian conquest in 604 B.C. (cf. Jer. 25:17-20).

Jeremiah's oracle on the Philistines compares her being overrun to a flood of waters coming out of the north. An army is to destroy her (Jer. 47:1ff.) The conquering enemy is the sword of the Lord. Her allies of Tyre and Sidon are no help. Mourning rites (cf. Deut. 14:1) are of no help to the Philistines.

The Moabites. Jeremiah devotes a lengthy oracle against the Moabites (Jer. 48:1-47; cf. Num. 24:17) who are descendants of Lot and his older daughter (Gen. 19:37). Moab's prominent cities are mentioned as being in distress. Her god Chemosh goes into exile with priests and princes. No city will escape. A curse is uttered on the one doing this work of the Lord with slackness (Jer. 48:10). Moab has been complacent (settled on her lees—an image from the settling of wine). The calamity is near at hand and those about are called on to mourn. The inhabitants of her cities are called upon to come down from their glory and to sit upon the ground. The breaking of the horn is a symbol of destruction of power. Moab's pride and arrogance are her chief sins; but there is also her idolatry. She magnified herself against the Lord. It is the Lord who brings an end to Moab making her like a vessel for which no one cares.

The Ammonites (Jer. 49:1-6). The Ammonites have Lot and his younger daughter as their ancestors (Gen. 19:38). They and their god Milcom are blamed for displacing the people of Gad who in Moses' and Joshua's day were allotted territory east of the Jordan. Rabbath Ammon (the location of modern Amman in Jordan) is threatened as Israel regains the lost territory. Wailing is in order as Milcom, his priests, and his princes go into exile. The Lord is responsible both for the Exile and the promised restoration.

Edom. Jeremiah's oracle against Edom (Jer. 49:7-22) parallels that of the book of Obadiah. Despite the wisdom of her counselors, Edom will be stripped more thoroughly than grape gleaners strip vines or thieves strip a house. The calamity is compared to drinking the Lord's cup of wrath. The oracle speaks of hearing a messenger sent among the nations to summons them to battle against Edom. Her mountain fortresses will not save her. Her overthrow is like that of Sodom and Gomorrah. Her fate is compared to a lion's coming up out of the thicket of the Jordan against a strong sheepfold. The invader is compared in swiftness to an eagle while Edom in helplessness is like the heart of a woman in childbirth.

Jeremiah has over forty references to Edom. He sees only destruction for it comparable to that of Sodom and Gomorrah. In the time of Moses, Edom denied Israel passage through Edom's territory (Num. 20:14-21). The territory stretched 100 miles from the Brook Zered (Wadi el-Hesa) to Aqaba and covered both sides of the Arabah. The trade routes passed through Edom's territory. Edom was in the alliance convened by Zedekiah (Jer. 27:3, 6, 7). Some Judeans attempted to flee to Edom at the time of the destruction of Jerusalem (Jer. 40:11-12), but Edom is accused of participating in the destruction of Jerusalem (Ps. 137:7).

Damascus. The oracle on Damascus is the briefest of the oracles on the nations (Jer. 49:23-27). Damascus in her defeat is compared to a woman in childbirth. The famous city is forsaken; her young men fall in her squares. The Lord kindles a fire on her walls to devour the strongholds of Benhadad (her reigning kings [cf. 1 Kings 20:2ff.; 2 Kings 6:24; 8:7; 13:3; Amos 1:4]).

Kedar and Hazor (Jer. 49:28-33). Kedar is a nomadic tribe scorned by Jeremiah for their shaven temples (Jer. 49:32), a practice forbidden in Israel (Lev. 19:27). Kedar is the extreme east point in an earlier comparison (Jer. 2:10). Her tents, flocks, and camels are threatened. Nebuchadnezzar, considered as acting for the Lord, defeated Kedar in 599 B.C. Hazor is an unknown site, not the place north-west of the Sea of Galilee. These people make up a nation at ease without military fortifications. Perpetual desolation is threatened.

Elam (Jer. 49:34-39). Elam is east of the Tigris River with Susa as its capital in a territory now of Iran. Ezekiel also tells of its fall (Ezek. 32:24-25). The oracle against Elam is dated at the beginning of Zedekiah's reign. The Lord threatens to bring the four winds against her scattering her to the four winds as she is terrified before her enemies. King and princes will be destroyed, but a restoration of fortunes is also promised.

Babylon (Jer. 50:1-51:64). Jeremiah in a long oracle describes the fall of Babylon to the shame of her gods Bel and Merodach. The result is Israel's seeking the Lord. They are called on to flee out of Babylon to escape her calamity. Utter desolation is in store with all who pass by hissing at her. Nebuchadnezzar destroyed Israel, but now the Lord is bringing Babylon punishment as he had punished Assyria. The Lord's weapons of wrath have been brought out. Babylon is to be requited for her deeds. Babylon is to be overthrown as Sodom and Gomorrah; wild beasts will occupy her. The invaders are like a lion coming from the thicket of the Jordan.

The Lord is the one who stirs up the destroyers against Babylon. The prophet calls on the Lord's people to flee out of Babylon. Her fall is the vindication of Zion. The Medes are the Lord's instrument. The Lord who made the earth and who controls physical phenomena is the one who makes all things. His implement breaks in pieces all things in order to requite Babylon for the evil it has done. The nations are summoned to war.

Preparations for war are described. Babylon is a threshing floor ready to be trodden. Jerusalem describes what she has suffered; and the Lord takes up her cause. Babylon has become a horror. The whole land, including her images, is put to shame. It is all for what has been done to Jerusalem. Sheshach (KJV: Jer. 25:26; 51:41) is thought to be a cryptogram for Babylon of the type known as athbash where the Hebrew letters are given in reverse order. Babylon was taken by the armies of Cyrus led by Gobryas in October 539 and only gradually fell into ruin.

Jeremiah is said to have written this oracle of Babylon, entrusted it to Seriah the chief priest (cf. 2 Kings 25:18; Jer. 52:24) when he went with Zedekiah to Babylon (while Jeremiah chose to remain in Palestine), and he instructed him to read it in Babylon. He was then to bind a stone to it and cast it into the Euphrates River. The accompanying imprecation was to be, "Thus shall Babylon sink, to rise no more, because of the evil I am bringing upon her" (Jer. 51:64).

The Return to the Land

Jeremiah repeatedly promised that some Israelites and Judeans would return from exile (Jer. 3:17-18; 16:14-15; 23:7 29:10; 30:10-11; 31:1-8; 32:37). The Lord's heart yearned for Ephraim and he would have mercy on him (Jer. 31:20).

Judah and Israel would be united under one leader (Jer. 33:15-16).

The throne name "Zedekiah" meant "The Lord is righteous," but in actuality Zedekiah was not loyal either to the Lord or to his oath to Babylon. Jeremiah promises a righteous branch to David. The expectation of a righteous branch is further expounded in Zech. 3:8-9; 6:12.

The Lord would supply healing to the outcasts (Jer. 30:17) and there would be a multiplication of population (Jer. 30:19). That which was now lacking would be supplied: "You shall be my people, and I will be your God" (Jer. 30:22; cf. 31:1). There would be cleansing from sins and there would be forgiveness (Jer. 33:8).

Consolation

Jeremiah at the beginning of his career was called not only "to pluck up and break down, to destroy and to overthrow," but also "to build and to plant" (Jer. 1:10). This second aspect of his message was more pleasant to Jeremiah than the first (Jer. 17:16; 20:8-9; 28:1-6). Though to this point we have chiefly noticed the aspects of his ministry which show him as a prophet of doom, the constructive elements in his preaching are of great importance. Despite his pessimism about the present, Jeremiah is a prophet of hope.

While the removal of the existing order was necessary to make room for a fresh one, Jeremiah occasionally speaks as if there were still hope of avoiding the calamity. The "what if" is at all times a significant part of the prophetic oracle. "Amend your ways and your doings and I will let you dwell in this place," the Lord promises (Jer. 7:3, 5-7; cf. 22:1-4; 26:3, 12-13).

Circumstances being what they were, however, Jeremiah considered that the Lord was bringing a nation upon Jerusalem (Jer. 5:15); the Lord himself would fight against the city (Jer. 21:5). The complete victory of the Babylonians was the will of God; immediate capitulation by Judah would be the part of wisdom; and the resistance was catastrophic. God was using Babylon as a warrior might use his battle axe. Later when finished with Babylon, he used the Medes for the destruction of Babylon:

> You are my hammer and weapon of war; with you
> I break nations in pieces; with you I destroy king-

doms; with you I break in pieces the horse and his rider; with you I break in pieces the chariot and the charioteer; with you I break in pieces man and woman; with you I break in pieces the old man and the youth; with you I break in pieces the young man and the maiden; with you I break in pieces the shepherd and his flock; with you I break in pieces the farmer and his team; with you I break in pieces governors and commanders (Jer. 51:20-23).

Even after the destruction of Jerusalem had taken place, all was not hopeless. The potter could make the broken clay into another vessel as it pleased him; and in that same way God would do good to Israel (Jer. 18:1-11). A remnant would survive the Exile. The future of the nation lay in the good figs in Jeremiah's parable who were the people already in Babylon (Jer. 24:1-9). The Exile was not permanent but was only for seventy years (Jer. 25:11, 12; 29:10) after which there would be a restoration (Jer. 27:22; 29:10-14). Jeremiah's advice, in his letter to the exiles that they build homes, marry off their children, and seek the peace of Babylon (Jer. 29:5-7), was really advice of hope. Now that the Judeans were in exile, the role of Babylon in God's plan was different from that earlier depicted when Babylon was the destroyer. Prayer for Babylon and for peace was prayer for the people of God. "For I know the plans I have for you, says the Lord, plans for welfare and not for evil, to give you a future and a hope" (Jer. 29:11).

After the fall of Jerusalem Jeremiah rejected the opportunity proffered him to go to Babylon with the exiles. He still had a word for his countrymen in Judah. After Gedaliah, the Babylonian governor in Judah, had been murdered, when Jeremiah advised against flight to Egypt, he promised his countrymen that if they would remain in the land God would rebuild them (Jer. 42:10-12). As he saw it, Israel was not merely the victim of circumstances; she was under the control of God. It was this concept that gave hope.

Jeremiah is said to have written a book of consolation:

For behold, days are coming, says the Lord, when
I will restore the fortunes of my people Israel and

Judah, says the Lord, and I will bring them back to the land which I gave to their fathers, and they shall take possession of it (Jer. 30:1ff.).

However, his picture of the future is restrained when compared with the hyperbolic pictures of the transformation of nature pictured in Isaiah 2 or in Amos 9. In his picture, exiles of the calamities of 722 (Jer. 3:12-14), of 597 (Jer. 29:10-14), or of 586 (Jer. 50:4-5), and even those who were left behind after Gedaliah's murder (Jer. 42:10), could participate in the restoration. Chapter 31:2-6, 15-22 is addressed to Ephraim which is a name for the northern tribes. Jeremiah speaks of a return from exile more wonderful than the Exodus from Egypt (Jer. 16:14-15; 23:7-8). There will be prosperity for both Israel and Judah (Jer. 31:27-28). Jerusalem is to be rebuilt (Jer. 31:38-40). There will again be pilgrimages to Jerusalem (Jer. 31:6) and laughter will be in the villages (Jer. 30:18-20; 33:10-13). The Lord will look upon the exiles for good and bring the people home (Jer. 24:5-7). The restored situation, however, is different from the pre-destruction one in that God gives the returnees a heart to know him (Jer. 24:7). It is into this picture that the doctrine of the new covenant fits. The old covenant—that made at Sinai—is broken in Jeremiah's view. There is no effort to reestablish Israel on the old basis.

A Field in Anathoth (Jer. 32:1ff.)

In the tenth year of Zedekiah (586 B.C.), in the darkest hour when the army of Nebuchadnezzar was besieging the city of Jerusalem and when Jeremiah was being held prisoner in the court of the guard for saying that the Lord would give the city to the Babylonians and that Zedekiah would be taken to Babylon, Jeremiah was informed by the Lord that a relative named Hanamel would offer him the privilege of redeeming a field (cf. Lev. 25:23-25; Ruth 2:20; 4:3-6) in Anathoth which he should buy and sign the deeds. Jeremiah did not know whether he had actually heard the voice of the Lord, or was merely suffering delusions, until the relative came. He says, "Then I knew that this was the word of the Lord" (Jer. 32:8). Jeremiah bought the field as instructed, paid the money, and signed the deeds, and then Baruch stored them in an earthen vessel for safekeeping (Jer. 32:9-14).

Perplexed at why good hard money should be spent at what appeared such a hopeless time, the prophet prayed and received the answer that his action was a symbolic act. Though indeed Jerusalem would fall to the Babylonians because of its idolatry, a day would come in which men would again buy fields and sign deeds in the country (Jer. 32:16, 42-44). The Exile was not the end of everything as far as Judah was concerned.

The parallel of this act of Jeremiah to an act carried out in Rome during the wars with Carthage has often been pointed out. Though severely threatened, the people of Rome were so confident of ultimate victory over Carthage that a prisoner brought into the presence of Hannibal while he was encamped outside of Rome reported that the very ground on which Hannibal was encamped had sold in the marketplace in Rome that day at no decrease in its ordinary value. So with Jeremiah, even the darkest hour of Jerusalem had an element of hope.

The New Covenant

Most distinctive of Jeremiah's hope is his doctrine of the New Covenant. Jeremiah previously makes specific references to the covenant only in 11:8, 14:21, and 31:32; but the terminology of the covenant, "I will be your God and you shall be my people," is elsewhere present (Jer. 7:23; 11:3-8; 24:7). Jeremiah's indictment of his countrymen had as its basic contention their failure to keep the covenant made from Sinai. The terms of the agreement made there were: "I will be your God and you shall be my people." In bringing about the Exile, God was revoking the covenant. However, in Jeremiah's preaching, the Exile was temporary. There was a remnant who would survive. A new covenant with Israel and Judah is to be made. Jeremiah does not suggest a negating of the revelation at Sinai. He does not suggest the giving of a new law. That from Sinai is sufficient, for the problem is not that the law is defective but that the people have not kept it. The first law was written on stone; but this new one is to be written on hearts.

Jeremiah having earlier said (Jer. 17:1) that sin is cut into their hearts of stone with a diamond pointed pen, here the heart becomes a palimpsest with God's word written on it (cf. Ps. 40:8) to become effective in the life. The formula of the new covenant is the same as the old covenant: "I will be to them a God and they shall be to me a people." All from the least to the greatest will know the Lord. Jeremiah does not promise a state of sinlessness, but promises forgiveness. Jeremiah's use of the term "new covenant" is the only use of the term in the O.T., but the idea is taken up by the writer of the Epistle to the Hebrews (Heb. 8:8-12; 10:16-17).

Jeremiah has stressed that the heart is deceitful and desperately corrupt (Jer. 17:9). It is in need of washing (Jer. 4:14); it is uncircumcised (Jer. 9:25). He promises a changed heart (Jer. 31:31-34; 32:38-41). Later Ezekiel enlarges this same suggestion to a doctrine of a new heart (Ezek. 36:25-27).

Jesus and Jeremiah

There are many parallels between Jesus and Jeremiah. The weeping over the slaughtered children of Bethlehem is explained by an appeal to Jer. 31:15 (cf. Matt. 2:18). Some people of Jesus' day saw him as a possible returned Jeremiah (Matt. 16:13-14). When Jesus cleansed the temple "house of prayer" came from Isaiah (Isa. 56:7), but it was with words about a "den of robbers" which had first been used by Jeremiah (Jer. 7:11; cf. Matt. 21:12-13; Mark 11:17) that the corruption of the people is explained. When Jesus took bread and the fruit of the vine at the Last Supper, he pointed to a fulfillment of Jeremiah's new covenant (Matt. 26:28; Luke 22:20; 1 Cor. 11:25). Through Jesus the forgiveness which Jeremiah envisions becomes a reality. Paul also appeals to the new covenant concept (2 Cor. 3:2-18), and it is discussed in the Epistle to the Hebrews (8:6-13; 10:16f.; cf. Rom. 11:27).

A Righteous Branch to David (Jer. 23:5-6; 33:14-17)

Jeremiah envisions that a remnant would survive to be regathered from the lands of exile in an act more marvelous than the Exodus from Egypt. He envisions a return from Egypt as well as from Babylon (Jer. 44:28) and there being faithful shepherds. In particular, he speaks of the righteous branch (*tsemach tsadiq*) for David (Jer. 23:5; 33:15; cf. Isa. 11:1ff.) which is a hope to be attached to Nathan's promise to David (2 Sam. 7:12-15) of a dynasty. The prophet Zechariah later took up the name "Branch" for the Messiah (Zech 3:8; 6:12). Zedekiah, then occupying the throne in Jeremiah's day, had a throne name meaning "Righteousness of the Lord," but his actions belied the name. The coming ruler is one worthy of the name: "The Lord is our righteousness." In another passage Jeremiah speaks of a return of David himself (Jer. 30:9), no doubt to mean one like David. The N.T. appeals to this expectation (Luke 1:32-33).

Jeremiah's promise of a restoration and of a future for Judah is expressed in language that is extremely strong. There is to be a return from exile, a repopulation of the land, a descendant of David on the throne, and Levitical priests offering sacrifices (Jer. 33:14-26; cf. Num. 25:13). If God's covenant with the night which maintains the sequence of night and day can be broken, then his covenant with David and the Levites can be broken (Jer. 33:19-21). At the same time, Jeremiah's promise of a return of one of a city and two of a family should not be overlooked (Jer. 3:14). Neither should the conditional nature of prophecy (Jer. 18:7-10) be forgoteen.

New Testament writers saw the fulfillment of the expectation of a descendant of David on the throne in the coming of Jesus to occupy the throne of his father David (cf. Luke 1:32, 69). At his exaltation to the right hand of God, Jesus occupied his throne there to sit until all enemies are destroyed, the last of which is death. When death is destroyed, then he will render the kingdom to God the Father that God may be all in all (1 Cor. 15:25-28).

Questions for Discussion

1. What role does Nebuchadnezzar play as described by Jeremiah?

2. What alternatives did Jeremiah offer the Judeans?

3. How does Jeremiah use the illustration of the potter?

4. What was Jeremiah's advice to those in the Exile?

5. Why did Jeremiah not go to Babylon?

6. What is the import of Jeremiah's most optimistic act?

7. What contrasts of the heart does Jeremiah offer?

8. What is Jeremiah's most influential concept?

9. What are Jeremiah's Messianic concepts?

10. How did Jeremiah end up in Egypt?

Chapter IX

LAMENTATIONS

Historical Background

Nineveh fell under the attack of the combined forces of the Medes, Scythians, and Babylonians in 612 B.C., and its refugees fled westward. Momentarily an Assyrian rump state was formed by Ashur-uballit with headquarters at Haran; but the battle of Carchemish in 605 B.C. (see Jer. 46:2, 10; 2 Chron. 35:20) spelled the doom of that state. At the same time, the battle also determined that Egypt, which supported Assyria in the battle and which itself had continuous expansion ambitions, would not move into the vacuum left and again rule the Middle East. Egypt, which previously had been an enemy of Assyria, had changed sides and had become an ally of Assyria in Assyria's final struggle against Babylon. But the battle was catastrophic not only for Assyria but also for Egypt; her days as an effective world power were over. Following Pharaoh Neco's defeat when he went to aid Assyria at Carchemish, Judah passed under the domination of Nebuchadnezzar, king of Babylon, from which it never escaped.

Because of Judah's repeated rebellions, the dismemberment of the Judean state by the Babylonians came in stages, but came swiftly. With the shift of domination of the area from Egypt to Babylon, King Jehoiakim had become a vassal to Nebuchadnezzar. In circumstances of which we know nothing, Daniel and his companions were carried off to Babylon in 606 B.C. (Dan. 1:1-6), the third year of Jehoiakim. In a few years Jehoiakim revolted and the revolt brought Nebuchadnezzar westward on a punitive expedition. Jehoiakim's death under unknown circumstances put his eighteen year old son Jehoiachin on the throne; but three months afterward, Jehoiachin capitulated to Nebuchadnezzar and was carried to Babylon along with ten thousand captives including the artisans of Judah (2 Kings 24:1ff). Among these captives was the prophet Ezekiel who later prophesied in Babylon to the exiles there. Nebuchadnezzar has left his own account of his campaign against

Jack P. Lewis   **87**

Jerusalem at this time which establishes March 15/16, 597 B.C., as the date of his capture of Jerusalem.

Mattaniah, another son of Josiah, was now placed on the throne of Judah by the Babylonians and was given the name Zedekiah. Zedekiah was a loyal vassal of Babylon for a few years, but eventually was enticed into a revolt by the pro-Egyptian party at his court. Nebuchadnezzar again came west, took Jerusalem in 586 B.C., demolished the walls, destroyed the temple, and exiled the significant Judean people, leaving behind the poor. The capture of Jerusalem in 586 is described in these words:

> In the fifth month, on the seventh day of the month—which was the nineteenth year of King Nebuchadnezzar, king of Babylon—Nebuzaradan, the captain of the bodyguard, a servant of the king of Babylon, came to Jerusalem. And he burned the house of the Lord, and the king's house and all the houses of Jerusalem; every great house he burned down. And all the army of the Chaldeans, who were with the captain of the guard, broke down the walls around Jerusalem. And the rest of the people who were left in the city and the deserters who had deserted to the king of Babylon, together with the rest of the multitude, Nebuzaradan the captain of the guard carried into exile. But the captain of the guard left some of the poorest of the land to be vinedressers and plowmen (2 Kings 25:8-12).

During the city's last years, Jeremiah, though not mentioned in the Book of Kings (cf. 2 Chron. 35:25; 36:12, 21, 22), was at the height of his career as a prophet, and in Babylon during that same time Ezekiel, beginning in 592 B.C., uttered his warnings to the exiles there. Not only were people exiled in 586 B.C., but also in Nebuchadnezzar's twenty-third year, which would be 582 B.C., other people were taken (Jer. 52:30). We do not know the circumstances.

It is in the bitterness of this tragedy of Jerusalem—the most severe calamity of the Old Testament—that the book of Lamentations was conceived. Struck white-hot off the anvil, likely by an eyewitness of the calamity, the book pours out the grief of the nation. The writer alludes to the siege, the famine which accompanied it, the attempted flight of the king, the looting of the temple, the burning of both the temple and other important buildings, the destruction of city walls, the slaughter of leaders, the exile of the inhabitants, the expectation of foreign help which did not materialize, and Judah's later provincial status (cf. 2 Kings 25:1ff.; Jer. 39; 52).

Introduction to the Book

Though following the arrangement of biblical books in the Septuagint and the Vulgate editions, the book of Lamentations is traditionally classified by Christians as one of the five major prophets, the book is not really a prophetic book at all. It is a collection of five poems composed in the dirge (*qinah*) meter some of which belong to the literary category called the "communal lament." This category is common in the Psalms and in the prophetic books, but Lamentations is the only O.T. book composed solely of laments. David's lament over Saul and Jonathan (2 Sam. 1:17-27), though an individual lament rather than a communal lament, is an excellent example of the lament category.

Three of the poems of Lamentations (1:1; 2:1; 4:1) begin with *'ekah* ("how") which is the characteristic beginning of a Hebrew lament or funeral dirge. From this feature comes its Hebrew name *'Ekah*. The Talmud gives the title *Qinoth* ("dirges") to the book. This term *qinah* "lamentations/lament" is found in Jer. 7:29; 9:[9]10, [19]20; 2 Sam. 1:17; 3:33. In the Greek Bible the book is called *Threnoi* ("Dirges"), a term also found in the Greek of 2 Chron. 35:25. The Latin Bible carries a subtitle *threni, idest, lamentationes jeremiae prophetae*, and that subtitle is followed in our English title of the King James Version: "The Lamentations of Jeremiah." This title is carried also in the ASV and RSV but is dropped to "Lamentations" in the NIV and NRSV.

In the threefold division of the Old Testament books used by Jews, the book of Lamentations is classified in the third division (the Writings), and it follows Psalms, Job, and Proverbs. A subdivision in the Writings is the Five Scrolls (the *Megilloth*), and Lamentations is the third of the five scrolls: Song of Songs, Ruth, Lamentations, Ecclesiastes, and Esther. The Talmud gives yet a different sequence of books: Ruth, Psalms, Job, Proverbs, Ecclesiastes, Song of Solomon,

Lamentations, Daniel, and Esther. The Stuttgart Bible has the sequence Ruth, Song of Songs, Qoheleth, Lamentations, and Esther. These various arrangements remind us that the Bible is an anthology of inspired books compiled by men on different assumptions.

In the synagogue, it is traditional to read Lamentations on the ninth of the month of Ab (July-August) which is the day that commemorates the destruction of the temple both by Nebuchadnezzar (586 B.C.) and by Rome (A.D. 70) (cf. Jer. 30:1-2; 41:4-5; Zech. 7:1-5; 8:18). In liturgical reading, it is customary to repeat Lam. 5:21 after 5:22 to avoid ending on a despondent note. Liturgical Christian churches use the book in the service preceding Easter to lament the sufferings of Jesus.

The Greek manuscripts carry a heading "Lamentations of Jeremiah" as a title of the book, indicating that, though the book is really anonymous, the tradition that it was composed by Jeremiah arose quite early. This tradition explains the present position of Lamentations which follows Jeremiah in the Greek, Latin, and English canons. The tradition was likely suggested by 2 Chron. 35:25: "Jeremiah also uttered a lament for Josiah; and all the singing men and singing women have spoken of Josiah in their laments to this day." Josephus states that the dirge over Josiah was still extant in his day (*Ant.* 10:5.1 [78]), but it is now lost. The book we have, however, is not a lament for Josiah whose death was in 609 B.C., not in 586.

This tradition of the authorship of Lamentations plays a major role in the popular picture of Jeremiah as the weeping prophet though there are also sections in the book of Jeremiah itself (cf. Jer. 9:1; 14:17-18; 15:10-18) which speak of his weeping. The Septuagint version has an introduction to the book of Lamentations of unknown origin and not represented in the Hebrew texts which in translation says:

> And it came to pass, after Israel had been carried away captive, and after Jerusalem had become desolate that Jeremiah sat weeping, and lamented with this lamentation over Jerusalem and said . . . .

The Latin Bible adds: ". . . with a bitter spirit, sighing, and wailing." Also the Talmud declares, "Jeremiah wrote his own book, Kings, and Lamentations" (b. Baba Bathra 15a). This tradition of Jeremiah authorship is further reflected in the Targum of Jonathan to Jer. 1:1, and is adopted by numerous ones of the Church Fathers.

Despite these traditions, some modern students feel that the elaborate style of the book, which differs from Jeremiah's book, and the attitude expressed about looking for foreign help (cf. Lam. 4:17), make it impossible to accept the tradition connecting the book with Jeremiah who had repeatedly prophesied that the city would fall. This last difficulty is weakened if the poet is thought of as expressing the attitude of the people rather than his own hopes. Lamentations is not quoted or echoed outside itself in either the Old or New Testaments.

The book of Lamentations, quite artistically constructed, is composed of five poems (as there are five books of the law, five divisions of the Book of Psalms, five scrolls, and other fives). It is to be compared in structure to other Hebrew acrostic poems like those in the book of Psalms (cf. Ps. 119). Three of these poems in Lamentations are acrostics with twenty-two verses each which is equal to the number of letters in the Hebrew alphabet. The system may be a mnemonic device, or it may suggest completeness of Israel's sin as "from A to Z" would to us. In the second, third, and fourth poems, the stanza for the Hebrew letter *pe* precedes that for *ayin*. This is a reverse order for these two letters from that of the present Hebrew alphabet. However, despite the alphabet sequence in Lamentations 1 and Psalm 119, a Hebrew alphabetic inscription found at Isbet Sarta in Israel has the sequence of alphabet of the laments which suggests that such a sequence was once known. Psalm 119 is the outstanding example of alphabetic acrostic in the O.T., but acrostics are also to be seen in Nahum 1:2-8; Psalms 9-10; 25; 34; 37; 111; 112; 119; 145; and Proverbs 31:10-31.

Chapter three is also an acrostic, but, differing from the other poems, has three successive verses, each beginning with the same letter of the alphabet, giving it a total of sixty-two verses. The number of chapters of the book of Isaiah and the total number of books in the combined Old and New Testaments are also sixty-six each. How this last fact is really relevant to Lamentations is not obvious since the Old Testament of which Lamentations is a part has only thirty-nine books. Chapter five of Lamentations has twenty-two verses (as do chapters one, two, and four, but is not an acrostic arrangement. It is a prayer rather than an elegy. The acrostic nature of these poems cannot be duplicated in an English translation. Of the popular English translations only the NIV and NLT have a footnote that an acrostic is being translated.

The first three poems have three lines to each strophe except for 1:7 and 2:19 where there are four lines. The fourth poem has only two lines to each strophe. In the third poem each of three lines of each verse begins with the same letter of the alphabet. The fifth poem has only one Hebrew line to each verse. The poetic features show that the book has been constructed with studied care.

The *qinah* (dirge) meter in which the bulk of these poems are composed is distinguished by having a line of two *stichoi*, the first of which has three stresses while the second has only two. It is a meter used by Jeremiah 9:9f., Ezekiel 19, Psalm 84, and Amos 5:2. The fifth poem of the book favors a 3 and 3 stress pattern.

The book of Lamentations was likely composed in Judah shortly after the destruction of the temple in 586 B.C. That the book does not know of the reconstruction is thought to place it before 516 B.C. when the temple was rededicated. Scholars have often called attention to the similarity of motif of a coin struck by Titus after the capture of Jerusalem in A.D. 70. The coin depicts a weeping woman under a palm tree and has the caption *Judaea capta*.

Being a reflection on the resulting situation, the book has all the air of coming fresh out of the sorrows of the calamity by an eyewitness, and it places a religious interpretation upon that calamity. It asks, What is the meaning of the terrible calamities that have overtaken Judah between 608 and 586 B.C.? Has God further plans for Israel? Though the Middle East tended to link inseparably the fate of a god and his people, as the" Lament over the fall of Ur" (*ANET*, pp. 455ff.) reflects, and tended also to feel that a people fell because their gods were weaker than those of the enemy, here the calamity has not shattered faith in God. It was the sin of Israel and not the impotence of Israel's God that was responsible for the calamity.

Lament over the fate of Jerusalem began immediately after its fall. Eighty men came from Shechem, Shiloh, and Samaria with beards shaved, clothes torn, and bodies gashed bringing cereal offerings and incense to present at the temple of the Lord (Jer. 41:5). When the Exile was over and the temple was being reconstructed, men of Bethel came to Jerusalem to ask the priests and prophets if they should continue to mourn as they had done for many years (Zech. 7:1ff.; 8:18, 19).

While the images of Lamentations are graphic indeed, they describe a situation that Western people in the twentieth century have not had to face—their cities have not been destroyed, their children have not died in the famine (cf. Lam. 4:1ff.). Nevertheless, the book is not devoid of value for us.

Lamentations deals with a real fact of life, but it is a theme that we do not with gladness consider. No humiliation is comparable to that experienced when one finally comes to the dead-end of the sinful way he has been traveling. There is no escape; he must face the shame of the consequences of his own evil deeds. He can only cry out in grief at his folly, and, if penitent, can only say, "God be merciful to me a sinner."

While being an expression of grief at the horrors that had been experienced, the book of Lamentations is a confession which agrees with the prophets' judgment previously announced on the sin of the people. The day of the Lord had come upon them. Psalm 137:7 calls it "the day of Jerusalem." The writer says, "Our fathers sinned, and are no more; and we bear their iniquities" (Lam. 5:7), but does not seek escape by blaming fate, the times, or the guilt of others.

There is no expectation of a quick turn in the fortunes of Israel; nevertheless, there is hope that God's mercy is not at an end. The poet calls for penitent waiting for God's mercy (Lam. 3:22-26).

As the poet describes conditions, the prophets are blameworthy for false and deceptive visions and for failing to expose the sins of the people (Lam. 2:14). Now they have no vision from the Lord (Lam. 2:9). The fate of the city "was for the sins of her prophets and the iniquities of her priests" (Lam. 4:13).

The fortune experienced is from the Lord. "The Lord is in the right, for I have rebelled against his word" (Lam. 1:18). The poet asks, "Why should a living man complain, a man, about the punishment of his sins?" (Lam. 3:39).

Despite the suffering he describes, the poet has not lost faith in the Lord. His steadfast love never ceases (Lam. 3:22-24), a theme now made into a lovely song. The Lord is good to those who wait for him (Lam. 3:25). The Lord will not cast off forever (Lam. 3:31). The Lord reigns forever (Lam. 5:19).

The poet issues a call to repentance: "Let us test and examine our ways, and return to the Lord! Let us lift up our hearts and hands to God in heaven" (Lam. 3:40-41).

Questions for Discussion

1. How does the book of Lamentations differ from the prophetic books?

2. What is the poetic structure of this book?

3. What is the historical background out of which Lamentations apparently came?

4. What are some of the dashed hopes the poet alludes to?

5. Who is blamed for Israel's fate?

6. What are the conditions in Jerusalem as described?

7. What are some of the more impressive metaphors and similes used by the poet?

8. How does the poet see prophecy?

9. What use has been made of the author's statement of faith?

10. What disappointed hopes does the author reflect?

Chapter X

THE PROPHET EZEKIEL

The Historical Background of the Book

A detailed grasp of the historical and political setting of Ezekiel is an absolute requirement if the student is to understand the book of Ezekiel. Following the fall of Nineveh in 612 B.C., the remnant of the defeated Assyrian empire established itself at Haran under Ashur-uballet but was in its death throes until Nebuchadnezzar, crown prince of Babylon, was victorious over Pharaoh Neco at Carchemish in 605 B.C. Neco had come to aid Assyria. That battle determined that the Neo-Babylonian empire, not Egypt, would be Assyria's successor in control of the Middle East. Egypt's hopes for expansion were at an end.

Within Judah, the death of Josiah at Megiddo in 609 B.C. in a vain attempt to stop Neco's advance to aid Assyria had put Jehoahaz (Shallum), Josiah's son, upon the throne; but Neco, only three months later, removed him and carried him a prisoner to Egypt. Neco then placed Jehoiakim (Eliakim), another son of Josiah, upon the throne. Then with the rise of Nebuchadnezzar to the throne of Babylon, lordship over Judah passed from Egypt to Babylon. Hostages from Judah like Daniel and his companions (Dan. 1:1ff.) were taken to Babylon.

After a brief period of vassalage, Jehoiakim saw fit to rebel against Nebuchadnezzar. Nebuchadnezzar came west to put down the revolt, but Jehoiakim died in unknown circumstances before the siege began. His son, Jehoiachin, after three months on the throne, capitulated to Nebuchadnezzar on March 15/16, 597 B.C., and was carried to Babylon along with the artisans and the upper classes of Israelites who were being exiled. Ezekiel the priest, the son of Buzi, was among them. Nebuchadnezzar has left behind an account, which was published only a few years ago, of his victory over Jerusalem.

Nebuchadnezzar placed Mattaniah, another son of Josiah, on the throne of Judah and gave him the name Zedekiah. Zedekiah, though at first a loyal vassal of Babylon, was by 586 into revolt, hoping to get aid from Egypt. The ensuing punitive action of Nebuchadnezzar brought to an end the Jewish state. The temple was burned; the wall of the city was destroyed, and Judah's people, except for the poor, were exiled. Gedaliah, left by Nebuchadnezzar to be governor over those still remaining in Judah, was murdered shortly afterward by Ishmael, and the surviving Judean people, hoping to escape further reprisals from the Babylonians, fled to Egypt taking Jeremiah with them. The long years of captivity had set in.

In the eleven years—the last years of the Judean state— following the calamity of 597, an undue optimism characterized those who had been left in Judah. They thought of themselves as the "cream of the crop" who had been left behind because of their virtues. They said of the exiles: "They have gone far from the Lord; to us the land is given for a possession" (Ezek. 11:15); but they said of themselves: "Abraham was only one man, and yet he got possession of the land; but we are many; the land is surely given to us to possess" (Ezek. 33:24). Ezekiel, like Jeremiah had done in his comparison of the two baskets of figs (Jer. 24:1ff.), sets the future hope of the nation upon those who are already in captivity; and the facts of the matter are that later those returning from exile were those who rebuilt the temple and not the "people of the land" who had never been in exile.

False prophets who promised them that the captivity would be over in two years (Jer. 28:1ff.) kept the exiled people in a state of extreme optimism and on the verge of revolt. This optimism seems to have centered around three focal points: (1) The people were Abraham's descendants and entitled to the promised blessings. (2) A descendant of David still reigned on the throne in Zion in the person of Zedekiah. God's promise of a perpetual dynasty to David had not been negated. (3) The temple where God's name dwelt was still standing in Jerusalem.

To combat this optimism which, if it led to revolt, would bring the doom of the people is the major goal of the first portion of Ezekiel's career. He insists that the expectation of a speedy return from exile is a delusion (Ezek. 13:1ff.). Zedekiah yet in Jerusalem was coming to Babylon (Ezek. 12:13-14) and the people still in Jerusalem would be dispersed.

On the other hand, when the final calamity came in 586 B.C. and Jerusalem was destroyed and the temple burned, a spirit of despair swept over the people which expressed itself in the phrases, "Our transgressions and our sins are upon us, and we waste away because of them; how then can we live?" (Ezek. 33:10); and "Our bones are dried up, and our hope is lost; and we are clean cut off" (Ezek. 37:11). Others use, "Our fathers sinned, and they are no more; and we bear their iniquities" (Lam. 5;7). To combat this despair, which if unchecked might lead to a complete abandonment of the Lord, is the aim of the second portion of Ezekiel's career. Ezekiel is the prophet of the Exile. For a nation to survive an exile and return to rebuild itself in its land is unique in history. Ezekiel is sometimes given credit for the survival.

The Prophet

The book of Ezekiel is represented by fragments of five manuscripts (1QEzek; 3QEzek; 4QEzek[a]; 4QEzek[b]; 11QEzek) and by quotations in other documents in the Qumran find (CD 3:20-4:2; 19:11-12; 4QFlor 1:16-17; 11QTemple 25, 27). Exiles were permitted a great deal of freedom with the exception that they could not return en masse to Jerusalem. What can be known of Ezekiel himself comes solely from his book. While the early part of his activity comes before the narrative of the books of Kings and Chronicles end, he is not mentioned in them. Ezekiel, whose name means "God is strong," was active in the twenty-two years from 592 B.C. (Ezek. 1:2) to 571 B.C. (Ezek. 29:17). Sizable portions of his book are in an autobiographical form; but actually, other than a list of his visions and symbolic actions, Ezekiel gives us little information about himself. Though he was a priest and was the son of Buzi, we know very little of him as a personality. He was active in Babylon. He had a house of his own and a wife who in the midst of his career was taken from him by death. These are the only private and domestic incidents to which he refers.

Ezekiel behaves in exceedingly strange ways, as we shall see, experiencing periods of immobility and speechlessness (Ezek. 3:26; 24:27; 33:22). Unlike Jeremiah who complained of his lot, if Ezekiel has emotional involvement in his work and any sympathy for his doomed people, it is expressed only in his cry, "Ah Lord God! will you make a full end of the remnant of Israel?" which he uttered when Pelatiah the idolater dropped dead (Ezek. 11:13). Ezekiel mechanically delivers his message that men may know that there has been a prophet among them and that it is the Lord who brings their doom.

Ezekiel's call to prophetic service is told in greater detail than that of any other prophet. At the same time, its details are so perplexing that many despair of the book before they get past the details. Ezekiel is distinctive in that he is the first prophet whom we know since Moses who was called to service outside of the land of Palestine. That call came at Tel-abib (Ezek. 3:15) in 592 B.C., five years after the calamity of 597 and only six years before the final end of the Judean state. By coincidence, a list of provisions for Jewish exiles has been found in excavations at the Ishtar gate of Babylon dating in this same year. Included in the recipients are King Yaukin (Jehoiachin?) of Judah and his sons. Ezekiel always dates events from the time of Jehoiachin's captivity. Ezekiel's years would partially be the years in which Jeremiah was active in Jerusalem. The thirtieth year mentioned at the beginning of the book (Ezek. 1:1) may be 568 B.C. and may be the dating of the book, but it is not the beginning of the prophet's career.

Ezekiel describes his initial vision ("visions of God"; cf. 8:3; 40:2) as arising out of a storm cloud. There were four living creatures and a chariot with wheels within wheels. More than forty uses of the number four are found in the book. The creatures seen have human, lion, eagle, and ox faces. The temple of Solomon was decorated with cherubs, and Babylonian palaces with composite creatures. The creatures are later used by the writer of the book of Revelation (Rev. 4:7). In trying to visualize what Ezekiel describes, I would suggest that one attempt to think of the appearance of a good West Texas norther with its boiling of clouds and its lightning. Ezekiel falls on his face in reverence before the glory of God but is raised up on his feet by the spirit. But most important of all, above this chariot was a chair and the likeness of a man upon it who could hand the prophet a scroll. As one reads the chapter, one will notice the extreme reluctance of the prophet to be specific as to just what he saw: "the likeness of a throne . . . and seated above it were as it were a human form." Lest we become lost in the details, this vision represents to the prophet the glory of God which was supposed to dwell in the temple in Jerusalem.

The distinctive idea of Ezekiel is that God's glory which had long been associated with the temple (1 Kings 8:11; Ps. 26:8; Ezek. 10:4; 11:23; etc.) can appear by the river Chebar, which is likely one of the canals near Nippur, south of Babylon. God could not be confined to Jerusalem or to the temple. He is no static national deity limited to one land and one people. He is the ruler of history. No nation lies outside his authority. In the wastes of Babylon, the Lord was present and had a word to say to his people through his prophet. His glory is not tied to one locality. It can abandon the temple and the city of Jerusalem (Ezek. 10:18ff.), leaving the people to their fate, and it returns only when the city has been rebuilt and cleansed (Ezek. 43:1-4).

From his vision the prophet is commissioned to go to a stubborn rebellious people (Ezek. 2:3) who are compared to briers and thorns (Ezek. 2:6) of whom he is not to be afraid; he is to preach whether they hear or refuse. They have a hard forehead and a stubborn heart, but he is to be harder against them. A hand stretched out to Ezekiel a scroll written on both sides with "lamentation, mourning, and woe" which at the Lord's command he ate. He found it in his mouth as sweet as honey, for the Lord's word is described elsewhere as sweeter than the drippings of the honeycomb (Ps. 19:10; 119:103; Jer. 15:16; cf. Rev. 10:9-10). This act is the symbolic impartation of the prophet's message to him (cf. Zech. 5:1; Rev. 5:1). His hearers were not those of foreign speech (Ezek. 3:4ff.) but yet were rebellious.

The prophet's task was an appalling one which left him speechless for seven days (Ezek. 3:15). He was awakened out of his stupor by the reminder that a watchman (cf. Jer. 6:17; Hos. 9:8; Hab. 2:1) once chosen must warn of the approaching danger; otherwise, he is responsible for the inevitable calamity. If the warning is sounded, then the watchman has discharged his task, and the responsibility for action rests upon the individual hearer (Ezek. 3:16f.; cf. Ezek. 33:1ff.). He was to warn both the sinner and the righteous (Ezek. 3:18-21). Ezekiel was told that he would be mute for a time (Ezek. 3:24ff.).

Ezekiel is addressed as "son of man" (cf. Ps. 8:4) some ninety-three times in the book. This term means a "human" as contrasted with the divine speaker who commissions him. In Ezekiel the term has no messianic import. "The word of the Lord came" (Ezek. 1:3; 7:1; 35:1) and "The hand of the Lord was upon me" (Ezek. 1:3; 3:14, 22; 8:1; 33:22; 37:1; 40:1) are Ezekiel's descriptive phrases to express divine control over him giving him his revelation.

The locale of Ezekiel's activities has been one of the most heatedly debated topics concerning his book. Since many of his visions are matters in Jerusalem which matters are described in extremely graphic details, some have attempted to have him reside there. Others have him being at times in Babylon and at times in Jerusalem. But since the prophet specifically says that he was in Babylon and that by the hair of his head he was carried in "visions of God" to Jerusalem; and since visions are just as real to the seer as the actual event, there seems little reason to insist that he was bodily in Jerusalem. He is a prophet of the Exile with a message for the exiles.

Ezekiel's generation found him quite amusing. They thought of him as a maker of allegories (Ezek. 20:49). They came to hear him as one might go to see a sideshow. They asked, "What are you doing?" (Ezek. 12:9; 24:19). They also said, "Come and hear what the word is that comes forth from the Lord" (Ezek. 33:30). They found him as one who sang love songs with a beautiful voice and who played well on an instrument. They heard what he said, but they would not do it (Ezek. 33:32).

The Message of Ezekiel

Ezekiel is a man of one idea: "Jerusalem must be destroyed." This is the one theme which Ezekiel has to speak upon in the first part of his career. The method of declaring it may have variations, but the theme remains the same. His theme is presented in symbolic act, vision, and allegory.

Symbolic actions on the part of the prophets are not at all limited to Ezekiel. Samuel's torn garment illustrated the split of the kingdom (1 Sam. 15:27-28). Ahijah tore a garment into twelve parts symbolizing the renting of the kingdom (1 Kings 11:29-39). Isaiah went naked and barefoot for three years (Isa. 20:1ff.). Jeremiah buried a linen loincloth and later recovered it. (Jer. 13:1-11). Few prophets, however, used symbolic acts more than Ezekiel did. These actions are a type of pantomime by which the prophet's message is graphically acted out. It has not been demonstrated that the action was thought to have magical quality to bring about the accomplishment of the prophecy as some interpreters have insisted that it did.

Ezekiel is led by the Lord to get himself a clay brick upon which he drew the city of Jerusalem and then played war by lying alternately on each side (Ezek. 4:1-8), three hundred and ninety days on the left and forty on the right. The three hundred and ninety days may be connected with the 393 years between the division of the kingdom and the fall of Jerusalem in 586 B.C. The Septuagint gives 150 and forty days respectively which is derived from the 150 years since part of the northern kingdom was exiled in 734 B.C. This act of Ezekiel was a symbol of the siege of Jerusalem by Nebuchadnezzar.

Ezekiel was called upon to drink water by measure (2/3 quart) only once a day and to eat sparingly by weight (8 or 9 ounces) once a day of food mixed of various grains (cf. 2 Sam. 17:28), cooked upon human dung as a symbol of the sparse, unclean food to be eaten in the siege. Human dung was ritually unclean (Deut. 23:12-14). In those dire times of Jerusalem people even turned to cannibalism (cf. Lev. 26:27-29; 2 Kings 6:24-30; Jer. 19:9; Lam. 2:20; Ezek. 5:10). Unclean foods are listed in Lev. 11:1-19. When the prophet protested that he had never eaten anything unclean (cf. Exod. 22:31; Lev. 7:22-27; 19:7; Deut. 14:21), the Lord permitted fuel of cow's dung (commonly used in the East) to be substituted for human dung (Ezek. 4:9-17).

The prophet was to shave his hair and divide the hair into three parts, one of which he burned, a second part he hacked to pieces with a sword, and a third he scattered to the winds, saving only a few hairs in his robe (Ezek. 5:1-17). This act symbolized various fates of the people in Jerusalem: death by pestilence and by the sword for some, and exile for others. Only a few were to be left to witness to the Lord's actions (Ezek. 12:16). The prophet charges that Judah had become more wicked than the nations about. He asserts that the Lord will act as he had never before and would never do again. He would vent his fury upon Jerusalem. It is all that "they shall know that God has spoken" (Ezek. 5:13).

In the midst of the account of symbolic acts, the prophet reports a command to prophesy against the mountains of Israel (Ezek. 6:1ff.). The Lord is bringing the sword against them which will destroy the idols and the people. The aim is the same as often stated: "You shall know that I am the Lord." Survivors are left scattered among the nations who will recognize that the Lord has done it.

Ezekiel is to clap his hands and stamp his foot while saying "Alas! ('ach; 6:11; cf. 25:3; 16:2; 36:2)" because of the abominations. The Lord is making the land desolate (Ezek. 6:11ff.).

The word of the Lord informs the prophet that an end has come on the four corners of the land (Ezek. 7:1ff.; cf. Amos 8:2). The oracle plays on the word "end." The Lord's eye will not pity. The day draws near. Wrath is on both buyer and seller. The Lord brings the worst of the nations to take possession. The Lord will judge the people and they will know that he is the Lord.

The prophet was commanded to prepare his luggage and to break out of the side of his house with covered head as a symbol of the fate of Zedekiah as he attempted to escape through the breach in the wall, but was captured, blinded, and taken to Babylon (Ezek. 12:1ff.). Ezekiel ate his food with fear and trembling as the people would do (Ezek. 12:17ff.).

To the people's accusation "The days grow long, and every vision comes to nought," the Lord assured Ezekiel, "None of my words will be delayed any longer" (Ezek. 12:21ff.). Ezekiel was told abruptly that the "desire of his eyes," his wife, would be taken from him but that he was to show no signs of grief. That evening his wife died (Ezek. 24:15-27). It was a sign for the people of the destruction of the temple: "the delight of your eyes, and the desire of your soul." Each of these actions caused the people to ask the reason for the prophet's strange behavior and gave him a chance to preach his message: "Jerusalem is doomed." Ezekiel was to experience a period of muteness until the news of Jerusalem's fall reached him (Ezek. 3:25ff.; 24:26, 27).

The visions of the book carry the same message as the actions. The prophet, while sitting in his house surrounded by the elders of Israel, a year and two months after his initial vision, was carried by his hair, and came to the temple to see its abominations which made certain that the temple and its worship could afford no security to the people (Ezek. 8:1ff.). In the north of the altar gate he saw an image of jealousy which was an idolatrous image of some sort. At the entrance of the court, after making a hole through the wall, he saw depicted on the wall pictures of creeping things and loathsome beasts with Jaazaniah and seventy elders offering incense to them. The participants were saying, "The Lord does not see us, the Lord has forsaken the land" (Ezek. 8:12); hence, they had turned to other gods. At the entrance of the north gate he saw women weeping over the fertility god Tammuz whose worship in the Middle East can be traced among the Sumerians as far back as 3,000 B.C. In the inner court at the door of the temple, he saw twenty-five men with their backs to the temple who were worshiping the rising sun. Although Josiah had destroyed the paraphernalia of sun worship (2 Kings 23:11), it had revived. These abominations made it obvious that God would neither accept sacrifice nor hear a prayer offered from the temple. Hope which centered in the temple was vain hope.

The prophet saw the six executioners of the city draw near (Ezek. 9:1ff.). But before the execution began, a man clothed in linen with a writing kit was commissioned by the Lord to put a mark on the forehead of all who sighed and groaned over the abominations of the city. The executioners were sent forth to slay indiscriminately and without pity the population who had no mark. They were to start with the elders and at the temple which was no longer an asylum (cf. 2 Kings 11:15). The people in their sin were saying, "The Lord has forsaken the land, and the Lord does not see" (Ezek. 9:9). The man doing the marking reported the completion of his task.

Ezekiel further saw the man in white linen commissioned to take coals from the wheel work of the vehicle that Ezekiel saw to sprinkle them over the city in a symbolic burning of the city. He saw the glory of the Lord in chariot form departing from the city that the city might be destroyed (Ezek. 9:3; 10:18; 11:22-23). While the prophet was prophesying, he saw Pelatiah, son of Benaiah, one of the twenty-five wicked counselors, drop dead (Ezek. ll:l3). Ezekiel cried out, "Ah Lord God! will you destroy all that remains of Israel in the outpouring of your wrath upon Jerusalem?" (Ezek. 9:8; cf. 11:13). The Lord rejected his intercession. The glory of God departed the city, going eastward to the mount of Olives (Ezek. 11:23). These visions make it clear that the hope in the continued existence of Zion is a delusion. Having seen the abominations in visions, Ezekiel was taken back in a vision to Chaldea to tell the exiles what he had seen (Ezek. 11:24-25).

False Prophets

Like Jeremiah, his contemporary in Jerusalem, Ezekiel had vigorous opposition from optimistic prophets who stirred the people to think that the captivity would soon be over. In chapters 13 and 14 he has strong things to say against them. They prophesy out of their own imagination following their own spirit when they have seen nothing (Ezek. 13:2, 3). Rather than standing in the breaches to repair the wall which had been broken by enemy attack, they are foxes undermining it. Using the prophetic formula, "says the Lord," they claim to give the word of the Lord when the Lord has not spoken. Furthermore, they use divination which is forbidden in Israel (cf. Deut. 18:14). Without their being sent by the Lord, they expect the Lord to fulfill their word.

They cry peace when there is no peace (cf. Jer. 6:14; 8:11). Instead of being true watchmen (cf. Ezek. 3:16-21; 33:1-6), they cover over defects with whitewash (Ezek. 13:10; cf. 22:28) which adds nothing to the wall's strength; but when the storm breaks, the wall will collapse. In modern terms one would say, "they cover up instead of cleaning up." The Lord threatens that he will tear down the wall and spend his wrath against those who whitewash it. These prophets have no share in the future (Ezek. 13:8, 9).

Ezekiel also decries those sorceresses who use magical charms to ensnare people like birds are ensnared (Ezek. 13:17-23). These charmers are not considered to be harmless cranks, but they have disheartened the righteous and have encouraged the wicked in his wickedness so that he did not turn from his way. The Lord will tear off their veils in order to save his people, so that the people "may know that I am the Lord." The equivalent of this phrase occurs eighty-six times in the book of Ezekiel and is one of its characteristic phrases.

Another attack upon the condition of the people which was bringing the calamity of exile is seen in the charge that the elders coming to inquire of the prophet come with idols in their hearts (Ezek. 14:1ff.). The temptation of people in exile far from the sanctuary in Jerusalem was to take up worship of the Babylonian gods alongside their allegiance to the Lord. One might expect that the Lord would give no answer to such inquirers.

As in the New Testament later the Lord threatens the sending of a strong delusion (2 Thess. 2:11), so here the Lord threatens the idolater with an answer which makes him an example and works his destruction (cf. Lev. 17:9; 20:3, 5, 6; Deut. 28:37).

Not only is the idolater threatened, but the prophet also. The Lord misleads the prophet (cf. Deut. 13:1-5; 1 Kings 22:19-23) and accomplishes his destruction along with the one who consults him. Then Israel will know that the Lord is the Lord. They will no longer be led astray but will be the Lord's people and he will be their God.

Ezekiel seems conscious of the fact that in religious matters a man accepts for some reason what he wants to believe. By rationalization one can convince himself that what he wants to believe is the will of God for him. One can see the process in operation when a person wants for some reason to do something that is wrong. At first he cannot bring himself to do it; but then he changes his mind and decides that it is not wrong after all. One said of a king of England that he always prayed because that gave him the courage to do the evil he was planning to do.

Individual Responsibility

There were those people in Israel who thought special mercy should be shown them because of the merit of the ancestors who had been righteous. Ezekiel said if there is famine, wild animals, sword, or pestilence in the land and Noah, Daniel and Job were in the land, they could not save sons and daughters by their righteousness. They could only save their own lives (Ezek. 14:12ff.).

But the prophet faced the responsibility problem in a second way. Some were saying, "Our fathers sinned, and are no more, and we bear their iniquities" (Lam. 5:7). This attitude seems to have expressed itself in a sarcastic proverb voiced not only in Ezekiel but also in Jeremiah (Jer. 31:29, 30). Jeremiah replies, "The teeth of everyone who eats sour grapes shall be set on edge."

Ezekiel considers various situations. First is the person who does that which is right (Ezek. 18:5-9). He avoids the common sins and follows the Lord's statutes. That person is righteous and will live. Judah's reigning house had seen such a person in Hezekiah who had carried through a great reform.

Next Ezekiel considers the son of the righteous man who turns from the righteousness of his father. Judah had seen such a son in the person of Manasseh for whose sake the decree of the destruction of Jerusalem had been given (cf. 2 Kings 21:11ff.; 23:26; Jer. 15:4). Ezekiel declares that the son will die for his own sin.

But there is also the son of the wicked father. Suppose the son turns from the sins of his father, will he die for what his father did? Judah had such a person in Josiah (son of Amon) who carried out the great reform of 622 B.C. (2 Kings 22-23). Ezekiel affirms that such a son will live.

Ezekiel next deals with the wicked man who decides to turn from his wickedness. Has his past wickedness created a pattern that he cannot break out of? Ezekiel answers that God has no pleasure in the death of the sinner. Such a person will live. Finally, he takes up the case of the righteous man who turns to wickedness. Such a person will die in his sins and all his righteousness will be forgotten. The people protested that such was not fair; but Ezekiel answered that it was they who were not fair.

Ezekiel returns to this teaching of individual responsibility in Ezek. 33:10-20, declaring that either the wicked or the righteous can change. Judgment is according to one's way. Paul later taught that each shall give an account to God for deeds done in the body (2 Cor. 5:10).

A further distinctive doctrine of Ezekiel is expounded in chapter 20. God acts "for the sake of his name." He was tempted to destroy Israel in Egypt, in the desert, and even in Canaan, but he was concerned with the nations getting a wrong impression of his power. Rebels will now be purged out. The promised return from exile is also for "the sake of his name."

Questions for Discussion

1. What are the years of the prophet Ezekiel?

2. What are some of the strange actions of the prophet?

3. Compare Ezekiel's attitude toward his task with that of Isaiah and Jeremiah toward theirs.

4. What problems confronted Ezekiel?

5. How did Ezekiel receive his message?

6. What is the audience's reaction to Ezekiel?

7. In what literary forms did Ezekiel convey his message?

8. How does Ezekiel describe opposing prophets?

9. What is the role of the prophet as seen by Ezekiel?

10. How is Ezekiel addressed and what is its meaning?

Chapter XI

EZEKIEL (2)

The Allegories

Under the form of numerous allegories, as he had done in symbolic acts and in visions, the prophet presented his theme that Jerusalem must be destroyed. Some of the allegories are explained in detail; however, for their comprehension a minute knowledge of the politics of the time is essential.

The earliest known Egyptian allusions to Palestine (those of Pepi and Sinuhe) describe its grape vines ($ANET^3$, 228, 18). Their prevalence in the country make that plant particularly suitable to be a symbol of the Israelite nation. This figure is used in both the Old Testament (Judg. 9:8-13; Ps. 80:8-16; Isa. 5:1-7; Jer. 2:21; Hos. 10:1) and the New Testament (Matt. 21:28-46; John 15:1ff.). To Ezekiel, the vine is the worthless wood out of which one cannot even make a peg. After the vine is burned at both ends and in the middle, that is, after the nation has suffered the calamity of 597 and has yet to face that of 586, it is hopeless (Ezek. 15:1-8). In Ezekiel, fire is the figure for destruction (Ezek. 5:2, 4; 10:2; 16:41; 23:47; 24:10-11). The land will become desolate (cf. Ezek. 6:14).

In another allegory, Israel is the foundling girl who has been reared and taken for a bride by the Lord, only to turn to harlotry (Ezek. 16:1ff.). Hosea (2:1ff.) and Jeremiah (2:2) use the marriage relation to show Israel's relation to the Lord; and Jeremiah 3:6-14 uses unfaithfulness as a figure for Israel's sins. Ignoring any period in the past when things were right between Israel and the Lord, Ezekiel stresses Judah's pagan background. Her father was an Amorite and her mother a Hittite (Ezek. 16:3). The clothing, the jewelry, and the food which the Lord supplied were used on the high places. The children were sacrificed to idols. Israel trafficked with the Egyptians and the Assyrians.

Ezekiel uses harlotry as a figure both for idolatrous worship and for political intrigue. Chapter 16 centers on cultic aberrations. More lustful than any other woman, Israel hired her lovers despite the fact that the universal practice is for the man to pay the woman (Ezek. 16:30-34). The fate of the harlot is in store for Judah (Ezek. 16:35-43). Her lovers gather against her. The punishment is death (Lev. 20:10; Deut. 22:22; Ezek. 16:40).

The proverb "like mother, like daughter" applies. Jerusalem came from pagan background—Amorite and Hittite. Her sisters were Samaria and Sodom. In the light of Jerusalem's sins, those of Samaria and Sodom seem righteous. The faults of Sodom are given:

> Behold this was the guilt of your sister Sodom: she and her daughters had pride, surfeit of food, and prosperous ease, but did not aid the poor and the needy. They were haughty, and did abominable things before me; therefore I removed them, when I saw it (Ezek. 16:49, 50).

The oracle ends with a picture of restoration in the new age (Ezek. 16:53-58). There is the promise of the enduring covenant.

A related theme is expounded in the allegory of the two adulterous sisters (Ezek. 23:1ff.; cf. Ezek. 16:45-46) who had one mother. Whereas in chapter 16 adultery was cultic aberration, here adultery is the political alliances in which the two nations engaged. The prophets opposed alliances with foreign nations.

Already in Egypt in their youth the two sisters—Oholah who is Samaria and Oholibah who is Jerusalem—had played the harlot. Oholah lusted after the Assyrians and did not abandon the prostitution of her youth in Egypt. The Lord turned her over to the Assyrians who stripped her and killed her (Ezek. 23:1-10). This section alludes to the fate of the northern kingdom, 735-722 B.C., when Samaria was taken by Sargon.

Her sister Oholibah saw her fate, yet she went further in harlotry (Ezek. 23:11ff.). After lusting after the Assyrians, she also lusted after the Chaldeans and had relations with them. She then turned to the Egyptians (cf. Jer. 37:5, 7) as she had in her youth. The threat is that the Lord will turn her over to the Babylonians for punishment, and they will strip her of her fine clothing. Her dependence on Egypt is to be destroyed. She must drink the cup (that is, share the fate) of her sister.

The Lord decrees that the two are to be turned over to a mob for punishment. The mob will stone them, cut them down with swords, and burn their houses. The allegory depicts a reaction to the entangling political alliances of the kings and with the idolatry the alliances brought with them. Judah is presented as more guilty in the Lord's sight than Samaria who had suffered her doom 130 years before. Ezekiel in these chapters uses extremely plain language in describing the perversions of harlotry.

The vulture allegory (Ezek. 17:1ff.) presents Nebuchadnezzar as a colorful vulture who has taken the top of the cedar and carried it off. The top of the cedar is to be understood as Jehoiachin who was taken to Babylon in 597 B.C. (2 Kings 24:10-17). Nebuchadnezzar then planted a cedar, that is, he put Zedekiah on the throne. Zedekiah is depicted as a low vine. He remained dependent on Babylon, for Nebuchadnezzar was his support.

A second vulture, not as elaborately described as the first, is Pharaoh Hophra (588-569 B.C.) who enticed the cedar toward himself (cf. Jer. 37:5). The allegory is interpreted in vv. 11-21. Mattaniah's name had been changed to Zedekiah which means "righteousness of the Lord." In his dealings with Egypt, Zedekiah had broken the loyalty oath to Nebuchadnezzar which had been sworn in the name of the Lord. Thus the prophet threatened the disloyal king with reprisals from Nebuchadnezzar for his breach of the covenant made with him.

Verses 22-24 interpret the allegory (fable) in a Messianic way with the Messiah being the twig set out.

An additional national symbol—the lion symbol—best known to us from the phrase "Lion of the Tribe of Judah" is called upon by the prophet as he presents the tragedy of the reigning house in a lion allegory. The meter of the section is the lament meter like that used in the book of Lamentations or that used in the chants at the death of a leader by professional mourners (Jer. 9:17). The lioness (who must be Judah) had trained her sons to catch prey; but the first, Jehoahaz, had been captured by the hunters and taken to Egypt (2 Kings 23:31-34) where he died. His fate is lamented in Jeremiah (22:10-12).

Jehoiakim is passed over in silence and the poem deals only with exiled princes. The second lion cub, likely Jehoiachin, had been put in a cage and taken to Babylon. Jehoiachin had been taken by Nebuchadnezzar in 597 B.C. Both Jehoahaz and Jehoiachin each had reigned only three months.

A second section (Ezek. 19:10-14) uses the vine image where the vine produces numerous stems, but they are broken off leaving no scepter for a ruler. The fire consumes Judah's branches. It is a lamentation (cf. Ezek. 32:16).

All of these allegories of the book of Ezekiel make quite clear that no hope is to be placed in the reigning house. The fact that a son of David was still on the throne of Jerusalem gave no security. Jerusalem is doomed.

The Foreign Nations

Like several prophetic books, Ezekiel also gives attention to foreign nations in a special section of his book. Though Ammon, Moab, Edom, and Philistia are mentioned (Ezek. 25:1ff.), it is Tyre and Egypt which are of special interest. The doom of Tyre is envisioned. Her fall is presented under the form of a great ship laden with precious cargo which founders in the midst of the sea (Ezek. 27:1ff.). There is a lament over the king of Tyre (Ezek. 28:11-19). Sidon which gets only a brief oracle is also condemned (Ezek. 28:20-23).

Doom for Egypt is also seen. Egypt is presented as a great dragon in her Nile River free from danger but who shall be captured; or Egypt is presented as a cedar well-watered which must be brought down to Sheol. She had been a seductive force to Israel: "A staff of reed (cf. 2 Kings 18:21; Isa. 36:6) . . . when they grasped you with the hand, you broke, and tore all their shoulders; and when they leaned upon you, you broke, and made all their loins to shake" (Ezek. 29:6, 7). Few better descriptions could be imagined for the way Egypt stirred up rebellion, promised aid, but never delivered. Nebuchadnezzar carried out a campaign against Egypt, but history has not preserved a clear record of its outcome.

The Future in Ezekiel

When Ezekiel's wife died (Ezek. 24:18) and the fugitive from Jerusalem arrived in Babylon after some delay to report that the city had fallen (Ezek. 33:21), the warnings the prophet had been giving had become a tragic reality. A spirit of despair comparable to that expressed in Ps. 137 set in, threatening to destroy the future of the people. While they said, "Our transgressions and our sins are upon us, and we waste away because of them; how then can we live?" (Ezek. 33:10), and "Our bones are dried up, and our hope is lost; we are clean cut off" (Ezek. 37:11), Ezekiel did an about face in his preaching and became a prophet of comfort. This second phase of his work presents the vision of the valley of dry bones that come to life (Ezek. 37:1ff.). There would be a rebirth of the nation. They would come out of their graves of exile. He joined two sticks upon which were written "Judah" and "Joseph" in his hand to make one stick—a symbol of the restoration of both halves of the nation (Ezek. 37:16). These pictures express the idea of a miracle to take place which is beyond all expectation. A return from exile is also projected in Ezek. 11:17; 28:25-26.

The prophet not only envisioned external renewal but spoke of inward regeneration. The nation would be cleansed. God would take away their old heart of stone and give them a new heart and a new spirit which would be responsive to his will (Ezek. 11:19; 18:31; 36:24-28). Though a great deal of emphasis is upon God's grace in the renewal, the prophet did not overlook the need for inward repentance on the part of the individual.

In this future, the Messianic hope also is not absent. Ezekiel alludes to it upon several occasions. The vulture allegory (Ezek. 17) ends in the Lord's planting a sprig of cedar that will bear fruit. The joined sticks (Ezek. 37:24-28) will have "My servant David" as king over them. The prophet indicts the present reigning house as evil shepherds who have looked after their own interests and have permitted the flock to be scattered (Ezek. 34:1ff.). God promises to become the shepherd to gather the scattered sheep. We recognize this passage as the ultimate source of the Good Shepherd figure used by the Lord in John 10. It is also an excellent statement of the duties of a pastor of God's people. This motif is picked up by Augustine (*City of God* 18:34). In Ezekiel, the parable ends with "my servant David shall be prince among them" (Ezek. 34:23-24).

Gog of the Land of Magog

Chapters 38 and 39 of Ezekiel are the object of unlimited speculation about what is going to happen in the future. In studying Ezekiel it is usually easier to admit that one does not know what these chapters are all about, and then pass on to other matters. I admit frankly that many times I have struggled with the question and the speculations and then have just given up. What they say seems clear enough; but what they mean is another matter.

Ezekiel, addressed in the usual term "Son of man," is told to turn his face toward Gog of the land of Magog, the chief prince of Meshech and Tubal, and to prophesy against him. It is stressed that God is completely in control of what happens. He turns Gog like a beast with hooks in its jaw (38:4). Gog is described as the leader of a great coalition which comes against the land which is restored from war, "the land where people were gathered from many nations upon the mountains of Israel." They "advance, coming on like a storm, . . . like a cloud covering the land" (v. 9; cf. Jer. 4:13). This army is composed of "horses and horsemen, all of them clothed in full armor, a great company, all of them with buckler and shield, wielding swords" [v. 4]. The description may be compared with that given in Ezekiel 23:12 for the soldiers that Oholibah (Jerusalem) doted on.

This army not only had Gog but includes Persia, Cush, Put, Gomer and all his hordes, and Beth-togarmah from the uttermost parts of the north (vv. 5, 6). This proud force said, "I will go up against the land of unwalled villages; I will fall upon the quiet people who dwell securely, all of them dwelling without walls, and having no bars or gates" (v. 11). The aim of the invaders is "to seize spoil and carry off plunder; to assail the waste places which are now inhabited, and the people who were gathered from the nations, who have gotten cattle and goods, who dwell at the center of the earth" (v. 12; cf. Judg. 9:37). The invaders are confronted by Sheba and Dedan and the merchants of Tarshish and all its villages who hope to get gain from the plunder (v. 13).

Ezekiel has the Lord to be the one who stirs up this host in the latter days (Ezek. 38:16). They come out of the uttermost parts of the north and are riding on horses; as a mighty army they come up against Israel like a cloud covering the land. God brings this host up so that the nations may know him when he vindicates his holiness through Gog (v. 16).

God has spoken of Gog in former days through his servants the prophets (cf. Jer. 4:5ff; Zeph. 1:14ff.) who had prophesied that God would bring up Gog (Ezek. 38:17; 39:8). However, God's wrath (cf. Deut. 32:22; Ps. 18:[9]8) is kindled by Gog's coming. At the great shaking, all creatures of the air, sea, and land (fish, birds, beasts, creatures, and people; cf. lists of Gen. 9:2; 1 Kings 4:33; Job 12:7-8) will quake, and mountain cliffs and every wall will be thrown down at God's presence (Ezek. 38:20). God will summon every type of terror against Gog. Panic will break out so that the invading warriors attack each other with their swords (v. 21). Meanwhile God will rain torrential rains, hailstones, and fire and brimstone, thus showing his greatness. "Then they will know that I am the Lord" (vv. 22-23).

Though God brings Gog up against the mountains of Israel, he will strike Gog's bow from his hand, and Gog and all his hordes will fall there. No agency with which God will accomplish this victory is hinted at. Israel is not said to fight them. The scavenger birds and the wild beasts will devour the corpses. The Lord will send fire on Magog and on those who dwell securely in the coastlands (Ezek. 39:1-6). God will not allow his holy name to be profaned any more. The nations will know that he is the Holy One of Israel (v. 7).

The people of the cities of Israel will burn the abandoned weapons: "shields, bucklers, bows and arrows, handpikes and spears." The abundance is such that for seven years, they will not need wood from field or forest. In this way they despoil those who despoiled them and plunder those who plundered them (vv. 9-10).

The place for the burial of Gog and all his host is made in the "Valley of the Travelers," east of the Dead Sea. The valley will then be called "the Valley of Hamon-gog" ("the multitude of Gog"). The KJV rendering, "It shall stop the *noses* of the passengers" (Ezek. 39:11; *chosemeth hi' 'eth-ha`obherim*; *BDB*, p. 340; *KBS*, p. 338; cf. Deut. 25:4—muzzle ox) is a conjecture borrowed by David Kimchi. The ASV has "It will stop them that pass through," and the RSV "It will block the travelers." The unburied defile the land (Deut. 21:23). Israel will be occupied seven months in burying the dead in order to cleanse the land. Especially set apart men will then search for yet unburied bones, and will set up a sign by any bone found that it may be buried in the valley. A city of Hamonah ("Multitude") will be there also. In this way the land will be cleansed (vv. 11-16).

This great victory is also presented in the image of a great sacrificial feast of the Lord. All the birds and beasts are invited to come to a great feast on the mountains of Israel. There they eat the flesh of the mighty and drink the blood of princes of the earth who are compared to sacrificial animals: rams, lambs, goats, and bulls from Bashan (vv. 17-18; cf. Deut. 32:14; Ps. 22:12; Amos 4:1). There the birds and animals will eat their fill of "horses and riders, with mighty men and all kinds of warriors" (vv. 19-20). Fat and blood of the sacrifice were ordinarily the Lord's (Lev. 3:17; Ezek. 44:15), but is here for birds and animals.

All nations will see the Lord's glory in this judgment which he has executed, and Israel will know that the Lord is "The Lord their God." "The nations will know that the house of Israel went into captivity because of their iniquity." The Lord dealt with them according to their uncleanness and their transgressions. The phrase "that they may know" is characteristic of Ezekiel (20:42; 28:24; 36:23; 37:28).

This bizarre section of Ezekiel ends with a promise of restoration of Israel. The Lord will be jealous for his holy name. Israel will be restored and will forget their shame when they dwell securely in their land with none to make them afraid. God gathers them out of enemy lands. God sent them into exile and will restore them to their lands and they will know that he is the Lord their God. He will not hide his face from them any more when he pours out his Spirit upon the house of Israel (vv. 25-29; cf. Ezek. 11:19; 36:26-27; 37:14).

A. Sources

Ezekiel in this passage has made use of numerous motifs which are found in earlier literature of the Bible. First is that of the Day of the Lord in which the Lord manifests his wrath. Next is the enemy out of the north (Ezek. 38:6, 15; 39:2) which is prominent in the earlier chapters of Jeremiah (1:13; 4:6ff.; 6:1ff; 6:22-23; 8:16; cf. Joel 2:20) and in Zephaniah (Zeph. 2:13). In Jer. 25:9 and Ezek. 26:7 this foe is Babylon.

Yet another motif is that of the onslaught of enemies to be defeated by the Lord (Joel [4]3:9ff.; Pss. 46, 48, 76; Isa. 17:12-14; Zech. 12:4; 14:3).

There are also less prominent motifs. The attack upon those who dwell securely has features in common with the Danites' attack upon Laish which they then named Dan (Judg. 18:7ff.). The panic in which the invaders kill each other is like that which struck the Midianites at Gideon's attack (Judg. 7:22) and the Philistines in Saul's war with the Philistines (1 Sam. 14:20). The Lord's use of enemy armies for his own purpose but then punishing them when they overstep their commission is expounded about Assyria in Isaiah (Isa. 10). Physical manifestations like the earthquake are common in theophanies of the O.T. (Judg. 5; Mic. 1; etc.). Rain as an element in the defeat of an enemy is seen in the defeat of Sisera by Barak (Judg. 5:21). Fire and brimstone is in the overthrow of Sodom (Gen. 19:24). The putting of a hook into the jaws to turn the enemy about is in the poem of 2 Kings 19:28 describing Sennacherib's invasion. It is also used in Ezekiel 29:4 for Pharaoh of Egypt. The sacrifice-feast motif is in Jer. 46:10 describing the battle of Carchemish and in Isa. 34:5-8; cf. Lam. 2:21f. It is in Zeph. 1:7 in his day of the Lord description. Plundering the defeated enemy's camp is seen in 2 Kings 7:1ff.

B. Later Influence

As Ezekiel used earlier motifs in order to deliver his message, so also the writer of the book of Revelation borrowed from Ezekiel. Following his description of the binding of Satan, the writer says:

> Satan will be loosed from his prison and will come out to deceive the nations which are at the four corners of the earth, that is, Gog and Magog, to gather them for battle; their number is like the sand of the sea. And they marched up over the broad earth and surrounded the camp of the saints and the beloved city; but fire came down from heaven and consumed them (Rev. 20:7-9).

However, this scene is not the only one borrowed from these chapters by the writer of the Book of Revelation. The great supper of God to which the birds of heaven are invited (Rev. 19:17-21) is also from this source.

C. Interpretation

Thus far these chapters are simple enough; but the problem begins when we begin to ask for identities of the participants. Other than in these two chapters of Ezekiel and the Book of Revelation, Gog occurs in the Bible only in a genealogy as the name of a Reubenite (1 Chron. 5:4) which case is not relevant to our problem. Numerous theories attempt to identify Gog. One connects him with Gyges, a king famous in Lydian exploits (*ca.* 670 B.C). Another attempts to connect him with Gugu of Lidi found in Assyrian texts. Still another tries a connection with Gogaia in a Tel Amarna letter. The *Qur'an* (Sura 18:90ff.) has Alexander the Great to build a wall around Gog and Magog. There are also mystical interpretations in which Gog is darkness and Magog the land of darkness.

Magog, Tubal, and Meshech in Gen. 10:2; 1 Chron 1:5 are the names of figures descended from Japheth, son of Noah. Meshach, Tubal, and Togarmah are places Tyre traded with (Ezek. 27:13). As the passage stands in Ezekiel, Magog merely means "from the land of Gog." But then we have Meshech and Tubal which are probably to be located east of Asia Minor and possibly to be identified with Phrygia and Cappadocia. Persia offers no problem. Cush is thought to be Ethiopia and Put to be Libya. Gomer (cf. Gen. 10:2—oldest son of Japheth); the Cimmerians (Greek for Armenia) and Bethtogarmah (a son of Gomer [Gen. 10:3]; Armenia) are in the area controlled by Turkey.

The effort to identify these invaders is almost as old as Ezekiel himself. Josephus (*Ant.* 1.6.1 [123]) and Jerome (*P.L.* 25:256) identified them with the Scythians who according to Herodotus (1:104) broke out of the Caucasus region and joined the Medes and the Persians in overthrowing Nineveh (612 B.C.). They then pressed on to the border of Egypt where they were bought off by Psammeticus I. Afterwards they took Ashkelon and ruled it for many years. Other people have attempted to identify the invaders with the Romans, the Goths, Napoleon I, Hitler, and most any other figure who threatened the peace of the world. Rabbinic literature offers other speculation.

The crucial issue is what to make of the Hebrew phrase *nesi' ro'sh* which the English Bible renders "chief prince of Meshech and Tubal" (Ezek. 38:2; 39:1). A small point of Hebrew grammar is the first issue to consider. The form of *ro'sh* is the same in the absolute and construct states. If *ro'sh* is taken as a noun in the absolute state, we have "prince of Rosh, Meshech and Tubal" as given in the American Standard Version and REB. The ASV then gave the alternate interpretation in the margin: "chief prince of Meshech and Tubal." If *ro'sh* is taken as a noun in the construct state, we have "chief prince of Meshech and Tubal" as in the KJV, RSV, NRSV, and NIV. *Ro'sh* is often used in the Old Testament for "head" or "chief." While one can appeal to the Greek (LXX, Symmachus, and Theodotion: *epi Gog kai ten gen tou Magog, archonta Ros, Mesoch kai Thobel*), to the Latin (*principen capitis Mosoch*), and to the Masoretic accents to support his case, there is no objective, definitive way by which one side of this dispute can convince the other side.

In the last century, a scholar, taking *rosh* as being in the absolute state and as being a geographical name, proceeded conjecturally to identify *ro'sh* with Russia. He then found Tubal to be identified with Tobolsk, a Russian city, and Meshech with Moscow. These identifications which would not be accepted by any scientific scholar today have appealed to dispensational premillennialists and are set forth by them as what the Bible actually teaches about the future. The notes of the Scofield Bible (p. 883) say, "That the primary reference is to the northern (European) powers headed up by Russia, all agree." The sermon topics like "Will Russia Invade the Middle East?" and other similar ones are based on the above mentioned conjecture. Likewise all the uneasiness about Russia's plans which are felt by these people are based on this questionable exegesis. If, however, *ro'sh* means "chief" in this setting and is not Russia (and I do not think it is), then the whole case falls to the ground.

The people mentioned were on the fringes of the world known by Ezekiel. The next issue is that of literal or figurative interpretation. One writer declares, "Gog and Magog symbolically represent the godless nations of the whole world." Dispensational premillennialism, however, claims as its trade mark the literal interpretation of all O.T. prophecy. When one looks at the system in detail, however, he finds in it an arbitrary mixture of literal and figurative interpretation. It is not at all clear how in the system one determines what is literal and what is figurative.

Certain acute problems arise in the literal interpretation of Ezekiel 38-39. Note the descriptions of the weapons used in the battle: "horses and horsemen, all of them clothed in full armor, a great company, all of them with buckler and shield, wielding swords" (Ezek. 38:4). "You and many peoples with you, all of them riding on horses, a great host, a mighty army; you will come up against my people Israel, like a cloud covering the land" (Ezek. 38:15-16). "Then those who dwell in the cities of Israel will go forth and make fires of the weapons and burn them, shields and bucklers, bows and arrows, handpikes and spears, and they will make fires of them for seven years; so that they will not need to take wood out of the field or cut down any out of the forests, for they will make their fires of the weapons" (Ezek. 39:10). "And you shall be filled at my table with horses and riders, with mighty men and all kinds of warriors" (Ezek. 39:20).

While all of these weapons and methods of warfare were suitable for Ezekiel's day, can any rational person really believe that in the future the nations (particularly Russia) will abandon jeeps, rockets, warheads, jet planes, and atomic bombs and go back to horse transportation and fight with "bows and arrows, handpikes, and spears?"

Ezekiel's Temple

Chapters 40-48 of Ezekiel tell of a vision seen by Ezekiel of a restored temple, of its priesthood and its service, of its people, and of the land in which it stood. Though technical, tedious, and foreign to the patterns of twenty-first century thinking, the narration is straightforward enough. Architects can plot out the design Ezekiel was talking about as one can see from drawings in any good Bible dictionary.

Nevertheless, there are few passages of the Bible which have perplexed people more about their interpretation through the centuries than have these chapters. They perplexed the ancient rabbis so much that they said that only Elijah, who in their theology would herald the final redemption, would elucidate them (b. *Men.* 45a). Rabbinic literature reports discussion about various books of the Bible in the early centuries. Hananiah ben Hezekiah before A.D. 70 is said to have saved these chapters of Ezekiel for the Canon of Scripture by taking three hundred jars of oil and burning the midnight oil until he had worked out for that time a satisfactory harmonization of them with the Pentateuch (*b. Hag.*

13a). In modern times most of the speculation that premillennialists engage in about a future temple to be built in Jerusalem rests upon the interpretation they give these chapters.

In the twenty-fifth year of the Exile in the tenth day of the first month (April 28, 573 B.C.), fourteen years after Jerusalem had fallen to the Babylonians in 587/6 B.C., the hand of the Lord took Ezekiel in visions of God (cf. 1:1; 8:2-3) and set him on a very high mountain (the temple mountain [Ezek. 17:22; Isa. 2:2; Mic. 4:2; Zech. 14:10]) south of which there was the city.

There he saw a man who looked like bronze but who had a measuring reed which was about ten feet and four inches long; he also had a linen cord for longer measurements. The man was Ezekiel's angel guide for his visionary visit to the temple (cf. Zech. 2:1; Rev. 11:1). The measurements taken are in cubits. The ordinary cubit was 17.5 inches and the older cubit which Ezekiel used was 20.68 inches.

Chapter 40 of Ezekiel describes the temple area, the three gates (east, north, and south) and the inner courts. The width and height of the wall was one reed. The eastern gate seems to be of the pattern with guard rooms of approximately the dimensions of foundations of gates of the Solomonic period found by archaeologists at Hazor, Megiddo, and Gezer. One ascended the first of three sets of steps in going into the temple area. The north gate had seven steps and came to the inner temple gate (Ezek. 40:22). There was also a gate on the south but none on the west. There were thirty chambers around the outer court (vv. 17-19). The space of the court was over 170 feet in width. Eight steps higher than the outer court was the inner court (v. 34). At the east gate leading into the inner court were the facilities for preparation of the sacrifices which were the burnt offering, the sin offering, and the guilt offering (vv. 38-43). On the north and on the sides of this one hundred cubit square inner court were buildings for the use of the Zadokite priests (vv. 44-47). The altar for burnt offerings stood in this square court and it is described in chapter 41:13-17.

The temple building itself was ten steps above the level of the inner court (Ezek. 40:49). There was a free standing pillar on each side of the entrance of the building (cf. 1 Kings 7:21). There was a vestibule ('ulam) which was twenty cubits (35 1/2 ft.) by twelve cubits (20 1/2 ft). The holy place was twenty cubits (35 1/2 ft.) by forty cubits (71 ft.), and the most holy which Ezekiel (though a priest) did not enter was twenty cubits (35 1/2 ft) in each dimension. Only the high priest (whom Ezekiel does not mention) entered the most holy place (Lev. 16:3ff.; Heb. 9:7).

This temple (*bayith*) was surrounded by three tiers of storage rooms reached by a stairway. There were thirty chambers per tier, making a total of ninety rooms which likely were used for storage of equipment and temple treasures. The temple building was not an assembly building and was quite small as public buildings go. West of the temple building itself was another building (Ezek. 41:12) the purpose of which is not explained.

The holy place was paneled with wood (cf. 1 Kings 6:15) and had recessed windows. The panels were decorated with carved likenesses of palm trees and cherubim each of which had two faces—one of a man and one of a lion (Ezek. 41:18). Ps. 92:[13]12 speaks of the righteous flourishing like a palm tree which likely is responsible for the palm tree motif. The holy place had an altar of wood 3.5 ft. wide and 5 ft. high which was a table before the Lord (Ezek. 41:22). Ezekiel does not mention the altar of incense or the lampstands which the tabernacle had. Both the holy place and the most holy had double leaf swinging doors which were decorated with carved palm trees and cherubim (Ezek. 41:24-25).

Chapter 42 describes the priest's chambers. Here the priests kept their clothing, ate their meals, and stored their share of the sacrifices. Ezekiel does not say anything about the high priest. The whole temple area was 500 cubits (861.63 ft.) square. In other words, it was just short of three football fields square.

Ezekiel had seen the glory of God leaving the temple by the east gate before the destruction of Jerusalem (Ezek. 10:18-19; 11:22-23). Now he sees it returning from the east with a sound Ezekiel compares to that of many waters (cf. Ezek. 1:24; Rev. 1:15; 14:2; 19:6). The glory comes to consecrate this restored temple (Ezek. 43:1-5). Ezekiel hears someone who is no doubt God himself speaking from the temple (Ezek. 43:6). The voice affirms that the temple is God's throne. The speaker points out the shame of placing the graves of the Israelite kings in the sanctuary; this desecration must cease (v. 7b). The NIV, in keeping with current redefinition (*KBS*, 911) given in the margin of the RSV, translates *peger* as "lifeless idols" (vv. 9, 10) and the REB as "monuments." The NRSV retains "corpses." God promises to dwell in the midst of the people of Israel forever (Ezek. 43:9). Ezekiel is commanded to describe the temple and its plan so that Israel will be ashamed of their iniquities. It is here that we seem really to get at the rationale of the vision.

The altar of the temple was of pyramid type composed of superimposed squares sixteen, fourteen, and twelve cubits each. One was two cubits and the other four in height. The altar steps (forbidden in Exod. 20:26 for the tabernacle) faced east. The altar's height was twelve cubits (20.68 ft.). It had four horns. The twelve cubits height and the twelve squares must have had some symbolic significance that is not explained. The priests of Zadok were to consecrate the altar with burnt offerings and sin offerings (Ezek. 43:18, 19).

The east gate of the temple was to remain closed since God had entered by it (Ezek. 44:1ff.). No foreigners, uncircumcised in heart and flesh, could enter (cf. Josh. 9:23; Num. 31:30, 47; Ezra 8:20; Zech. 14:21). The mass of Levites, because of their earlier idolatry, are to be temple servants but cannot be priests (Ezek. 44:9-14). The Levites who are sons of Zadok are to be priests, and their qualifications and services are described (Ezek. 44:15-31). Zadok supported Solomon while Abiathar supported Adonijah. With Solomon's coronation, Abiathar was banished to Anathoth, and Zadok was given the service of the priesthood (1 Kings 2:26, 27, 35). As an interesting sidelight, the Qumran community supported the Zadokites in their literature. Ezekiel describes the clothing of the priests, their hair, and their marriage laws. They act as teachers and as judges, and they are not to defile themselves for the dead. They get their living partly from the sacrifices and partly from estates assigned to them (cf. Ezek. 45:4-5). Nothing is said by Ezekiel of the high priest.

The land of Palestine is to be reapportioned. A district twenty-five thousand cubits (8.15 miles) long and twenty thousand (6.52 miles) broad is to be set aside as the Lord's portion of the land within which is the temple with a fifty cubit (86.16 ft.) square around it. Another section twenty-five thousand cubits long and ten thousand broad is to be set aside for the Levites. This whole area is 8.3 miles square. Then there is an area five thousand cubits broad for the whole of Israel. The prince is to have land on both sides of the holy district equal to one tribal district from the western to the eastern boundary of the land (Ezek. 45:7, 8). He is not to oppress the house of Israel (Ezek. 45:9). The identity of the prince remains unexplained. The whole arrangement is to safeguard the holiness of the sanctuary.

In this new arrangement there are to be just weights and balances (Ezek. 45:10ff.). The people bring token gifts to the prince and he offers them to God as their representative (Ezek. 45:13-17).

A sin offering is made on the first day of the first month of the year (Ezek. 45:18-20). The passover is on the fourteenth day of that month. Unleavened bread is eaten seven days. Then in the seventh month on the fifteenth day, a sin offering is made (Ezek. 45:25). This festival is also for seven days.

Chapter 46:1-8 gives regulations for the prince. He is to make an offering every sabbath and every new moon. Vv. 9-10 make provision for traffic in the sanctuary on the festivals. One must pass from gate to gate and not leave by the one through which he entered. Vv. 11-15 describe the freewill offering of the prince. Vv. 16-18 provide that crown property is not to be disposed of permanently. If given to a non-relative, it was returned at the year of liberty (Jubilee year; Lev. 25:8-17). Vv. 19-20 speak of the prince's quarters (see Ezek. 42:1-14). Vv. 21-24 describe the temple kitchens.

The angelic guide (cf. Ezek. 40:3) appears in chapter 47:1-2 for the last time. The visionary temple visit is ended. Chapter 47:1-12 describes the sacred river which is a motif also found in Joel 3[4]:18; Zech. 14:8; and Rev. 22:1-2). From below the threshold of the temple (which is called God's throne in Ezek. 43:7), the river flows east in increasing depths: ankle deep, knee deep, up to the loins, and then after four thousand cubits it is deep enough to swim in and could not be crossed. Trees were on each side of the river as the water flowed down through the Arabah to the Dead Sea. Though now 1300 ft. below sea level and containing water of 25% salt, the sea's water becomes fresh, has fish, and from Engedi to Eneglaim (Ein Feshkha ?) its shores become a place fishermen spread nets; however, the swamps and marshes remain salty as a source for salt needed for sacrifice (cf. Ezek. 43:24). The trees on the banks of the sea bear fresh fruit each month and their leaves are for healing.

In keeping with the oath made to Abraham (Ezek. 47:14; cf. Gen. 12:7; 15:17-19; 17:8) of perpetual possession of the land by Abraham's descendants, the boundaries (Ezek. 47:13-23) of the land are described. The boundaries are about those of David's empire except that trans-Jordan territory is not included (Ezek. 47:18). The north is set at the Entrance of Hamath (Lebo Hamath; possibly Lebweh, fifteen miles north of Baalbek; cf. 2 Sam. 8:5-12; Num. 34:7-9). The east is between Damascus and Palmyra along the edge of the desert. The south is from Tamar on the Dead Sea to Meribath-kadesh, fifty miles south of Beersheba in the southern Negev. From there the boundary goes to the Brook of Egypt which is fifty miles south of Gaza. The western boundary is the Mediterranean.

The land west of the Jordan is to be divided between the tribes with alien and Jew treated alike (Ezek. 47:22, 23). Without regard to geographical features of the land, the area is assigned in parallel strips running across the country from east to west. The sequence of tribes starting in the north is Dan, Asher, Naphtali, Manasseh, Ephraim (cf. Gen. 48:17-20), Reuben, and Judah. Then comes the strip in which the sanctuary is located. This section is twenty-five thousand cubits long and twenty thousand broad. The priests who are sons of Zadok have an allotment about it as do the Levites. Each territory is twenty-five thousand cubits long and ten wide which they cannot sell or exchange. The extra five thousand cubits is for ordinary use, and in its midst is the city which is 4500 cubits square (Ezek. 48:8-12).

South of the sanctuary area are the territories of Benjamin, Simeon, Issachar, Zebulun, and Gad (Ezek. 48:23-28). This plan places the children of Rachel and Leah nearer the sanctuary than those of the handmaids Zilpah and Bilhah.

The city which is 25,000 cubits square (cf. Rev. 21:16), already described in Ezek. 45:1-8, has three gates on each side named after a tribe (including Levi) but with Ephraim and Manasseh combined into Joseph (cf. Rev. 21:12-14). The name of the city is "The Lord is There" (*Yahweh-shammah* [Ezek. 48:30ff.] cf. the new name of Isa. 62:2). For other names, see Isaiah 1:26; 60:14; Jeremiah 3:17; Zechariah 8:3.

Meaning?

The temple described by Ezekiel is not exactly like that of Solomon, of Zerubbabel, or of Herod in its details. It is far too large for the top of Mt. Moriah and the platform Herod built there. Its service is not precisely that described in the Pentateuch for the tabernacle. The apportionment of the land described pays no attention to Palestine's geographical features. How are we to understand this vision? If the whole is to be taken literally, the topography of Palestine will have to be modified considerably.

Dispensational premillennialism claims as its distinctive trademark the literal interpretation of all O.T. prophecy. This system affirms that in the future we are to expect Ezekiel's temple to be constructed in Jerusalem. In fact, when the state of Israel was set up and the war of 1967 gave the Jews the control of the eastern part of Jerusalem, the first question some Christians asked the Israelis was, "When are you going to build the temple?" Contributions were offered from Christians to the government for this purpose. To help get the project on the road, a few years ago a disturbed man burned the El Aksa mosque which occupies a part of the temple platform in order to get the program underway.

The *New Scofield Bible*, after surveying other options says,

> The preferable interpretation is that Ezekiel gives a picture of the millennial Temple. Judging from the broad context of the prophecy (the time subsequent to Israel's regathering and conversion) and the testimony of other Scriptures (Isa. 66; Ezek. 6; 14) this interpretation is in keeping with God's prophetic program for the millennium. The Church is not in view here, but rather it is a prophecy for the consummation of Israel's history on earth (p. 884).

The objectionable aspect about this interpretation is that according to the teaching of the Epistle to the Hebrews, temple worship was abolished by God's own hand through the work done in Christ. To reestablish it would be to dishonor that work and its results. Sacrifice was temporary, and the whole system was a shadow of good things to come. The whole system has been done away. There was one sacrifice for sins for all time when the Christ died (Heb. 7:18, 19; 9:6-10, 28; 10:1-9). Worship in the heavenly sanctuary is based on the one sacrifice of Jesus Christ (Heb. 10:8-12).

The sacrifice for sin repeatedly mentioned in Ezekiel's vision has always been a great problem for those who would interpret Ezekiel's temple as something to be built in the millennial age. Scofield in the original edition of his work said:

> Doubtless these offerings will be memorial, look-ing back to the cross, as the offerings under the old covenant were anticipatory, looking forward to the cross. In neither case have animal sacrifices power to put away sin (Heb. 10:4; Rom. 3:25) (p. 890).

This comment is really a begging of the question. Scripture says nothing of such offerings being memorial. From the first century until the present the Lord's Supper has been the memorial of the offering of Jesus on the cross. Yet Scofield and his company would have us to think that in the future something else will be made a memorial. Scofield's interpretation is not a literal interpretation though literal in-terpretation is supposed to be the trade mark of the millennial interpre-tation. Scofield has supplied an element that Scripture knows nothing about.

The *New Scofield Bible*, published in 1967 to bring the notes up to date, continues to struggle with this question:

> A problem is posed by this paragraph (vv. 19-27). Since the N.T. clearly teaches that animal sacrifices do not in themselves cleanse away sin (Heb. 10:4) and that one sacrifice of the Lord Jesus Christ that was made at Calvary completely provides for such expiation (cp. Heb. 9:12, 26, 28; 10:10, 14), how can there be a fulfillment of such a prophecy? Two an-swers have been suggested: (1) Such sacrifices, if actually offered, will be memorial in character. They will, according to this view, look back to our Lord's

work on the cross, as the offerings of the old covenant anticipated His sacrifice. They would, of course,
have no expiatory value. And (2) the reference to sacrifices is not to be taken literally, in view of the putting away of such offerings, but is rather to be regarded as a presentation of worship of redeemed Israel, in her own land, and in the millennial Temple,
using the terms with which the Jews were familiar in
Ezekiel's day. (p. 888).

The same objections, previously mentioned, deal with the first option offered. The second one is a total capitulation of the case for literal
interpretation of O.T. prophecy, though it is not admitted to be such. If
the sacrifices are not to be taken literally, there is no reason at all to
take the temple and the rest of the description literally. There are basic
inconsistencies and elements of arbitrariness built into the millennial
case which cannot be harmonized.

Ezekiel saw the glory of God leave the temple in the sixth year of
Jehoiachin's captivity (Ezek. 10:18-19; 11:23) which would be 591 B.C.
The vision of the temple was nineteen years later in the fourteenth year
after the city of Jerusalem was smitten (Ezek. 40:1, 2). The date is long
before the return led by Zerubbabel in 536 B.C. The description includes appointments for the slaughter of victims. There are tables for
utensils with which to prepare the burnt offering and the sacrifice (Ezek.
40:38-43). The vision is likely a figurative pattern for the return period
and its worship. The purpose was to instruct the exiles concerning the
restoration. We have no information about the plan of the temple built
by Zerubbabel. The blessings promised through Ezekiel were conditional like those promised through Moses (Ezek. 43:10, 11).

The living waters of Ezek. 47, as well as of Zech. 14:8, were the
living waters of the Gospel (John 7:38). Jesus uses the expression. The
disciples assembled in the temple on Pentecost, and the Gospel went
forth from there (Mauro).

The temple of God has been under construction ever since the first
century. According to 1 Cor. 3:16, the Christian is the temple of God.
"What agreement has the temple of God with idols?" (2 Cor. 6:16).

Built upon the foundation of the apostles and prophets, Christ Jesus himself being the cornerstone, in whom the whole structure is joined together and grows into a holy temple in the Lord; in whom you too are built into it for a dwelling place of God the Spirit (Eph. 2:19-22).

Influence on the Book of Revelation

The Book of Ezekiel is a primary source from which the images of the book of Revelation have been drawn. A few of these cases include the sealing of the 144,000 (Rev. 7:1ff.; cf. Ezek. 9:4), the eating of the scroll (Rev. 10:9-10; cf. Ezek. 2:8-3:3), the great supper (Rev. 19:17-21; cf. Ezek. 39:17-19), Gog and Magog (Rev. 20:8; cf. Ezek. 38-39), the measuring of the city (Rev. 21:15; cf. Ezek. 40:3); and the river of life (Rev. 22:2-5; cf. Ezek. 47:1-12). There are numerous lesser motifs.

Questions for Discussion

1. What is Ezekiel's allegory of the grape vine?

2. In what way does Ezekiel allegorize God's bride?

3. How are the exchanges of kings depicted?

4. How does Ezekiel present Tyre?

5. How does Ezekiel present the rebirth of the nation?

6. What does Ezekiel do with the lion image?

7. What does Ezekiel mean by "for the sake of his name?"

8. What is Ezekiel's teaching of individual responsibility?

9. What problems are encountered in a literal interpretation of Ezekiel's temple.

10. What parallels does the book of Ezekiel have with the book of Revelation?

Chapter XII

DANIEL

Introduction

In the Greek, Latin, and English Bibles the book of Daniel follows Ezekiel and is the last book in the group called the Major Prophets, but in the Hebrew Bible where the books are arranged differently, the book follows Esther and precedes Ezra and Nehemiah as a portion of the third division of the books of the Bible—the division known as the "Writings" (called Hagiographa from Greek). The book of Daniel was known to the author of the *Sibyline Oracles* in a section conjecturally dated to the second century B.C. One fragment from Qumran Cave 4 uses the title "Daniel the prophet" as does the N.T. (Matt. 24:15). Daniel is not included in the Cairo codex of the prophets completed about A.D. 895. The Talmud handed on the tradition, "The men of the Great Assembly wrote Ezekiel, and the Twelve Minor Prophets, Daniel and the scroll of Esther" (*b. Baba Bathra* 15a). The Great Assembly is now thought to be mythical; hence, the tradition is only a curiosity.

The Hebrew-Aramaic book of Daniel is a book of twelve chapters; but Greek and Latin manuscripts add to these The Prayer of Azarias, The Song of the Three Hebrew Children, and the stories of Susanna and of Bel and the Dragon. None of the eight fragmentary manuscripts of Daniel from Qumran (1QDaniel[a]; 1QDaniel[b]; 4QDaniel[a]; 4QDaniel[b]; 4QDaniel[c]; 4QDaniel[d]; 4QDaniel[e]; 6QDaniel) contain these sections. The Catholic Bible follows the Latin manuscripts in including these stories; but non-Catholics reject them as being apocryphal since they are not in Hebrew. While all early English Bibles (including the first KJV of 1611) also translated these sections and printed them along with other apocryphal books in a section between the Old and New Testaments, they are now often published separately in collections of material called Old Testament Apocrypha. The TEV, NRSV, and REB can be obtained either with or without the Apocrypha.

Except for Codex Cigianus and the Chester Beatty Papyrus, Greek manuscripts contain Theodotion's text of Daniel which represents a Greek revision made in the second century A.D. rather than having the Septuagint text. It is assumed that this practice is due to the poor quality of the translation in this portion of the Septuagint. Printed Greek texts like Rahlfs' edition usually print the two translations with one on the upper half of the page and the other on the lower at the same opening.

The authorship of Daniel (cf. Dan. 9:2; 10:2) is one of the most heavily debated issues separating conservatives from liberal scholars. A Daniel is mentioned by his contemporary Ezekiel (Ezek. 14:14, 20; 28:3) as one renowned for his wisdom. However, it is now a widely held opinion that the Daniel of Ezek. 14:14 is to be identified with *Dan'el* of the Ugaritic texts of the 14th century B.C. The *Aqhat* legend of Ugarit tells of king *Dan'el* who "judges the cause of the widow, adjudicates the case of the fatherless" (*ANET*[3], pp. 149-55). Nevertheless, the relation of the Ugaritic figure to the central figure of the book of Daniel is not certain. Should the opinion that the Daniel of Ezekiel is the one of Ugarit rather than the one of the book of Daniel prove to be true, then all that can be known of the life and career of the Israelite Daniel comes from the book of Daniel itself. The name Daniel which means "God judges" is also borne by other Israelites (1 Chron. 3:1; Ezra 8:2; Neh. 10:6). The name also occurs in 1 Enoch 6:7; and there is a Daniel in Jubilees 4:20 who is uncle and father-in-law of Enoch.

The first six chapters of the book of Daniel, containing stories about Daniel and his three companions, are written in the third person while the last six which narrate Daniel's visions are almost entirely in the first person and mention Daniel only at 7:1, 15; 8:1, 15, 27; 9:2, 22; 10:7, 2, 11, 12 and 12:4, 5, 9. Daniel is instructed to seal the book until the time of the end (Dan. 12:9).

The New Testament attributes certain statements (Dan. 9:27; 11:31; 12:11) to the prophet Daniel (Matt. 24:15); but already in the third century (*ca.* A.D. 260) the Neo-Platonist Porphyry, who denied the possibility of predictive prophecy, asserted that the book of Daniel reflected events of the Maccabean age, a time much later than that in which Daniel lived. According to Porphyry the book was written after these events instead of predicting them.

Though the allegation was rebutted by the contemporaries of Porphyry, critical scholarship has now taken up that affirmation and insists that the book is of Maccabean date, arising out of the persecutions of Antiochus IV (Epiphanes) between 168 and 164 B.C. This position also assumes that there are historical inaccuracies in the book. Conservative scholars contend that the book is an authentic proclamation of the sixth century Daniel.

The book of Daniel has been handed down to us with the beginning and ending portions in Hebrew but with a portion in Aramaic in the middle. The Aramaic section is 2:4b-7:28. This shift is already attested in the Dead Sea Scrolls. Probably because of this Aramaic section, there is no Targum (Aramaic translation) to Daniel. The apocryphal additions earlier mentioned are from Greek.

The earliest extant texts of the book of Daniel are the eight fragments of manuscripts from the Qumran Caves. Two fragments of a manuscript of Daniel were recovered from Cave One, five are from Cave Four, and one from Cave 6. The *florilegium* (4Qflor) found in Cave Four referred to Daniel the prophet. 4QMelchizedek also has affinities with Daniel. These fragments attest the popularity of Daniel in the second century B.C.

While Daniel is not included in the honor role of the faithful of the book of Ecclesiasticus, Daniel's book is alluded to in 1 Maccabees 2:59-60, Baruch 1:15-2:3, and in the *Sibyline Oracles* 3:397ff., all from the second century B.C. It is likely that the *Sibyline Oracles,* ca. 140 B.C., contain the earliest extant echo of the book. There is also a close relation between 1 Enoch 14:18-32 and Daniel 9:7-18. There are allusions to the book of Daniel in the New Testament (Mt. 24:25; MK. 13:14) and use of it by the writer of the Book of Revelation. Josephus in the first century A.D. relates the story of the book at length (Josephus, *Ant.* 10.10.1-11.7 [186-281]).

The first part of the book of Daniel belongs in the literary category of "story with a moral." Like the book of Jonah, it does not contain prophecies by Daniel in the same way that the other prophetic books contain prophecies uttered by their respective authors; but the first six chapters contain a number of stories about Daniel and his friends. Then there are also the revelations made to Daniel in the last chapter. These features neatly divide the book into two divisions. The first contains a series of stories concerning the experiences of Daniel and his three companions (Dan. 1-6) while the second contains visions of Daniel (Dan. 7-12).

The Exile of Daniel and His Companions, 1:1-21

Following the battle of Carchemish in 605 B.C., Judah passed from Egyptian domination to Babylonian domination. A coming of Nebuchadnezzar to Jerusalem and an exile of Jews in the third year of Jehoiakim (606 B.C.; cf. Jer. 25:1; 46:2) is known to us only from the book of Daniel. 2 Kings 24:1; 2 Chron. 36:6-7 tell of Nebuchadnezzar's coming against Jehoiakim but do not give a date. In Daniel, vessels of the temple were taken to a temple in Shinar.

The exiles designated for governmental service were entrusted to the care of the king's eunuch Ashpenaz for three years. In Egypt, much earlier, Potiphar is described as a eunuch (saris; Gen. 37:36) as Ashpenaz is (Dan. 1:3). The term was a title, not necessarily implying castration. We have a later record found in excavations at the Ishtar Gate of Babylon of provision being made about 592 BC. (considerably later than the first chapter of Daniel) for royal exiles in the provisions made for Yaukin of Judah and his sons (ANET[3], p. 308).

Of the noble youths taken from Jerusalem, Daniel (whose name means "God is my judge") and his three companions—Hananiah, Mishael, and Azariah—each of whom has a theophoric name, were singled out for special treatment by the Babylonians. Supplied with the Babylonian names—Belteshazzar, Shadrach, Meshach, and Abednego (theophoric names from Babylonian gods)—the four purposed to maintain their religious integrity by refusing to transgress the dietary restrictions (Dan. 1:8). Hos. 9:3, much earlier, threatens that there will be unclean food in the Exile. Such food might include the prohibited foods (Lev. 11:2-47), food not free from blood (Deut. 12:23-24), and food previously offered to idols.

After requesting water to drink and vegetables to eat (the Hebrew word zero'nim/zero'im, translated "pulse" in the KJV, occurs in all known literature only in vv. 12, 16), at the end of the test period of ten days, the four proved superior to those who ate the king's dainties. We do not know the names of those other Hebrew young men involved beyond Daniel and his three companions. Rough parallels about concern for foods are in Tobit 1:10, 11 and Judith 12:2. The seven Jewish brothers and others of the Maccabean period (1 Macc. 1:62-63; 2 Macc. 5:27; 6:18-31; 7:1ff.) were tortured because they would not eat swine's flesh. The N.T. talks of meats offered to idols (1 Cor. 10:1-13: Rom. 14:1; Josephus *Life* 3 [14]). Jewish priests in Rome lived on figs and nuts.

At the end of ten days the Jewish boys in Daniel were in better condition than their associates. Though all the boys were wiser and more understanding than the enchanters and magicians of Babylon, Daniel had special skill also in the interpretation of visions and dreams.

The story stresses the motif that God honors the loyalty of his servants. Though Daniel went into exile with the first group of exiles, he lived on through the Exile until the time of Cyrus who permitted the first group of exiles to return to Jerusalem in 536 B.C.. Daniel continued longer until at least the time of Darius (Dan. 6:1).

Nebuchadnezzar's Dream, 2:1-49

The dream of Nebuchadnezzar, dated in his second year (that is, 604 B.C.), could not be interpreted because (KJV) the king himself could not remember its details. Modern translations interpret differently and have Nebuchadnezzar refusing to reveal the dream. In reply to his magicians' and others' insistence (cf. Dan. 2:4-11; 4:6-7) that his demand was unreasonable, Nebuchadnezzar ordered their execution as charlatans. The decree put Daniel and his companions under death sentence, but Daniel received the mystery of the king's dream in a dream of his own at night, and offered to interpret it. However, he, like Joseph earlier had done (Gen. 41:16), disclaimed any personal credit for his ability. Earlier examples of revelation by dream include those of Abimelech (Gen. 20:3), Pharaoh (Gen. 41:1ff.), and Solomon (1 Kings 3:5-14).

Nebuchadnezzar had seen a vision of a great image whose head was gold, whose breast and arms were silver, whose belly and thighs were bronze, and whose legs were iron and whose feet were mixed iron and clay. A stone cut out of the mountains smote the image to dust and the wind carried it off, but the stone became a great mountain and filled the earth.

Daniel explained that the image represented a sequence of four world empires beginning with Nebuchadnezzar. However, beyond that of Nebuchadnezzar, the identities of the empires are not given by Daniel. Daniel explained that "in the days of these kings," that is, during the fourth empire, the God of heaven would set up a kingdom, never to be destroyed, which would break in pieces these kingdoms. It, in turn, would stand forever.

Because of the skill Daniel had displayed, he was worshiped by Nebuchanezzar (Dan. 2:46), and he was elevated to be ruler over all the wise men of Babylon, and his three companions were appointed over affairs in Babylon.

The identity of the four empires is a major disputed question in the study of the book of Daniel. In order to have the book of Daniel focus on the Maccabean period, certain treatments like that of H.H. Rowley and that of the *Interpreter's Bible* identify the four empires with Babylon, Media, Persia, and Greece. However, history knows of no Median kingdom intervening between Babylon and Persia. The book of Daniel elsewhere considers the Medes and Persians together (Dan. 5:28). Our sources would establish that Cyrus followed without lapse of time on the heels of the Babylonian kings; hence, this case must assume that the writer of the book of Daniel was in error.

While conservative scholars recognize that there was no Median empire, some identify the fourth empire with the successors of Alexander the Great. They also have to assume that the everlasting kingdom section of the prophecy remains unfulfilled. Other scholars identify the fourth empire with Rome. The authors of Baruch and of II (4th) Ezra in the first century A.D. have the fourth empire to be Rome.

One of the crucial issues of current conservative discussion of Daniel is what is to be made of the assumed ten toes of the image (ch. 2:41-42), which are not specifically explained in Daniel, or what is to be made of the ten horns of the fourth beast in a later vision (ch. 7) in Daniel's time scheme.

The futuristic interpretation of Daniel makes great capital of the ten toes of the image, and either attempts to identify them with ten governments in Europe which it considers to be heirs of the Roman Empire, or postulates that the Roman Empire will be revived at the close of the ages in the form of a ten-nation confederacy under the leadership of the "Beast" or final world-dictator. This last case also holds that the stone will strike a final blow at the end of the age. It is asserted that nothing in earlier history has yet approximated the ten toes of the image.

A modification of this system attempted to identify the ten toes with the nations in the Common Market; but that system went awry when the Common Market expanded beyond ten nations. Since the text of Daniel does not specify the number of toes involved, the speculation would come out quite differently if one calculated twelve toes as the giant of Gath had (2 Sam. 21:20; 1 Chron. 20:6).

It is entirely arbitrary to find only ten governments in Europe! What is one to do with the others that exist? Furthermore, the system is out of joint in time perspective for if the toes represent either the present situation in Europe or a future situation, then the toes cover a greater period of time than all the rest of the image put together. The kingdom represented by the head lasted about seventy years, the shoulders about two hundred, the thighs about two hundred, and the legs about six hundred—a total of 1070 years. But the toes must represent about fifteen hundred years up to the present time.

But beyond these difficulties, the kingdom was "at hand" in the days of the Roman Empire (Matt. 3:2; 4:17; 10:7); was to be in the life of those then living (Matt. 16:28); was set up on the first Pentecost after Jesus' resurrection; and the Colossians were translated into it (Col. 1:13). Rather than being the major focal point of the whole scheme, the toes and the horns must be a part of the fourth empire and must reflect division in it. There is no material here for outlining in advance how history is yet to go.

The Image of Nebuchadnezzar, 3:1-30

Nebuchadnezzar's golden image, sixty cubits (90 feet) high and six (9 feet) wide, was set up in the plain of Dura with the decree that at the sound of musical instruments all must fall down and worship. The one who refused would be cast into the fiery furnace. Most ancient religions were broad-minded and had no problem with adding a new worship, but the Jewish religion was exclusive; hence, Jews refused to worship other deities.

Following the accusation of Shadrach, Meshach, and Abednego by the Chaldeans, the king sought to deliver them by giving them another chance to worship the image. Daniel is not a participant in this narrative. With admirable faith and courage, the three reply that if God is able to deliver them, he will; but even if he does not, they will not worship the image (Dan. 3:18). They are then condemned to the furnace. Though the fire was heated seven times hotter than ordinary, and, though those who threw them into the fire were killed by it, the three Hebrews were unharmed. The Epistle to the Hebrews speaks of quenching raging fire by faith (cf. Heb. 11:34). The king stated that he saw a fourth man who was like a son of the gods (that is a divine person) walking with them in the fire. There is no reason at all to identify this person with Jesus as some early Christians did and some modern ones do. The KJV has "like the Son of God." At the king's command the three came unharmed out of the furnace. The king admitted that God had sent his angel to deliver them, and he decreed that all must worship the God of Shadrach, Meshach, and Abednego.

The Dream of the Tree by Nebuchadnezzar, 4:1-37

A dream of Nebuchadnezzar, which his magicians, enchanters, and astrologers again could not interpret, was put to Daniel. He saw a great tree which reached to heaven, the beasts found shade under it, the birds dwelt in its branches (cf. Mt. 13:22), and all flesh was fed from it; but the decree went forth from heaven to cut down the tree and to leave the stump. It was to be wet with the dew of heaven. Its mind was to be changed to a beast's mind, and seven times were to pass over it. Whether years, months, or seasons are involved in the seven times one cannot know. Likely seven is symbolic for completeness. The lesson implied in the dream is to be completely learned.

After a long time Daniel was able to interpret the dream. He explained that the tree represented Nebuchadnezzar and that he would be driven from men to dwell among the beasts until he recognized that the Most High rules in the kingdoms of men and gives them to whomever

The Major Prophets

he wills. Daniel advised repentance that the sentence might be mitigated. The dream was a warning rather than an announcement of fixed destiny (Dan. 4:27).

In due time, after twelve months (Dan. 4:29), Nebuchadnezzar was saying, "Is not this the great Babylon I have built?" Indeed it was, and its remains today attest to its greatness! There were palaces, parks, canals, defenses, the ziggurat, and the famous Hanging Gardens which were considered one of the seven wonders of the ancient world. But Nebuchadnezzar was driven from his throne to eat grass like an ox, his hair grew like eagles' feathers, and his nails were like birds' claws until he acknowledged God. Afterward, his reason returned to him and he was established in his kingdom as before. The story underscores the truth that pride goes before destruction. The Babylonian Chronicles have no record of such an experience of Nebuchadnezzar, and it has been conjectured by many scholars that an episode in the life of Nabonidus, the last king of Babylon, has been retold in this story. Some scholars claim that this argument was underscored by the discovery in 1947 in the Qumran Cave 4 of a Prayer of Nabonidus (cf. *BASOR* 145 (1947):31f). Nevertheless, the case is entirely conjectural. Nabonidus is not mentioned in any biblical passage, but it is known from classical sources.

The Handwriting on the Wall, 5:1-31

Belshazzar's feast for a thousand lords made use of vessels brought by Nebuchadnezzar from the temple in Jerusalem (cf. 2 Kings 24:13; 25:15; Jer. 27:19-22). Nebuchadnezzar drank, became intoxicated, and praised the gods of gold and silver with the vessels. But a man's hand wrote on the wall opposite the lampstand, and the enchanters, Chaldeans, and diviners could not interpret the writing. While Nabonidus and Belshazzar had the first two places in the kingdom, the third is offered the interpreter. When none could interpret, the queen recalled that Daniel had ability in secret matters. When called, Daniel reminded the king that he had been impious in his use of temple vessels for a feast (v. 23).

The words on the wall were *Mene, Mene, Tekel,* and *Parsin.* When transposed into English tranliterated terms, these would be weights: Mina, Mina, Shekel, and Half-shekel. It would seem that Daniel took these nouns and made verbs (which in Aramaic are slightly different the days of Belshazzar were numbered. He had been found weighed in the balance and found wanting, and his kingdom was to be divided and given to the Medes and Persians. There may be a word-play between *paras* and *Persian*, the conquerors of Babylon.

Belshazzar's historical existence, once heatedly debated, has been abundantly established by occurrences of his name in cuneiform writings (see R.P. Dougherty, *Nabonidus and Belshazzar* [New Haven: Yale U. Press, 1929]). He was co-regent with his father (*ANET*[3], p. 313b). While we have no text which specifically attributed kingship to Belshazzar, his very existence is no longer in doubt as it once was. Three generations separate Nebuchadnezzar and Belshazzar who is son of Nabonidus. "Father" (cf. Dan. 5:2, 11, 18) in this case must be used loosely for "predecessor." The identity of the other character in the story, Darius the Mede, continues to be elusive to us. See H.H. Rowley, *Darius the Mede and the Four World Empires in the Book of Daniel* (Cardiff: U. of Wales Press Board, 1959), and J.C. Whitcomb, *Darius the Mede* (Grand Rapids: Eerdmans, 1959). Darius succeeds Belshazzar but is referred to as in the past in the time of Cyrus (Dan. 11:1).

The warning of the handwriting shortly came to pass. That night the king was killed. Xenophon, *Cyrophaedia* VII.5.1ff., and Herodotus, *History* I.191, tell of the fall of Babylon. The city was taken without a struggle in 539 B.C.. Cyrus in his famous cylinder represents himself as a peaceable conqueror (*ANET*[3], pp. 315-16; see also the *Nabonidus-Chronicle* [*ANET*[3], p. 306]).

Daniel in the Lion's Den, 6:1-28

When, under Darius, Daniel was exalted to be one of the three presidents over the one hundred twenty satraps, a case was sought against him. By this time he would have been more than eighty years of age. However, no case could be found other than his loyalty to God. To ensnare him, an unchangeable decree (cf. Esther 1:19; 8:8) was sought that no petition should be offered except to the king for thirty days; however, Daniel, with his window opened toward Jerusalem, prayed three times daily as usual. When the matter was brought to the attention of the king, though he desired to deliver Daniel, he found it necessary to enclose Daniel in the den of lions with the petition, "May your God whom you serve continually, deliver you!" (Dan. 6:16). An apocryphal writer composed an unbelievable legend of Habakkuk's being sent to take food to Daniel.

After the King's spending a sleepless night, at daybreak he found Daniel unharmed, for God had shut the lions' mouths (cf. Heb. 11:33). Daniel was brought unharmed out of the den. In retaliation, his opponents were cast in with their families and were overpowered by the lions before they reached the bottom of the pit. The outcome of the affair was a decree that all should fear the God of Daniel.

The stories about Daniel and his companions have as their chief aim the encouraging of a people to hold fast in times of persecution. If they will but endure, they will be triumphant.

Questions for Discussion

1. What form does the book of Daniel have?

2. What is the structure of the book of Daniel?

3. What was at stake about food in Babylon?

4. What is the most disputed question about the book of Daniel?

5. What are the strengths and weaknesses of various systems of interpreting Nebuchadnezzar's dream?

6. What is the faith of Daniel's companions?

7. How did Daniel interpret the handwriting?

8. What implications concerning pride are set forth in the book of Daniel?

9. How is the fidelity of Daniel praised?

10. What archaeological material is relevant to the study of Daniel?

The Major Prophets

Chapter XIII

THE VISIONS OF DANIEL

The Book

The second portion of the book of Daniel (Dan. 7-12) narrates four visions of Daniel in a form which set the pattern for later apocalyptic. In particular, the motifs of an angel explaining the vision and that of the sealing up of the book for later times are made use of by later writers.

The first portion of Daniel observes a general chronological order, and the visions of the second part are also related in chronological order but begin before the stories of the first part of the book end. Chapter 7:1-28 continues the Aramaic section of the book. Chapter 8:1 reverts to Hebrew.

The Dream of Daniel. Ch. 7

The dream, dated in the first year of Belshazzar (554 B.C., a date prior to that of the narratives of chs. 5 and 6), brought Daniel a vision of the stirring of the great sea by the wind and of four beasts of different appearances coming up out of the sea. While at first the symbolism of the vision may seem strange to us, we also represent kingdoms by animals; for example, the Russian bear, the Chinese dragon, and the British lion. Composite beasts of the sort here encountered were regularly used in Babylonian art and examples may be seen in collections of art and in archaeological objects.

The first beast was like a lion with eagle's wings, the wings were plucked off, and the lion stood on two feet like a human and was given a human mind. The second beast was like a bear with three ribs [NRSV: "tusks"] in its mouth and was commanded to devour many bodies. The third beast was like a leopard with four wings and four heads and dominion was given it. And then the fourth beast, different from all the others, is not compared to any animal. It was exceedingly strong and had iron teeth. It devoured but stamped with its feet what was left. The beast had ten horns, but then among the horns came another little horn with a mouth speaking great things, and it uprooted three of the horns.

While Daniel watched, one Ancient of Days, with clothing white as snow and hair like pure wool, sat on the throne which was fiery, and judgment began. Great multitudes stood about to serve him. The books were opened. The beast was slain and the dominion of the other beasts was taken away.

Daniel saw one like a son of man (that is, like a human) who came to the Ancient of Days [NRSV: "an Ancient One"] on the clouds of heaven and received dominion and glory and a kingdom that would not be destroyed. All people should serve him. Augustine commented on the dream (*City of God* 18.24).

The vision troubled Daniel, and, when he asked its meaning, he was told by his attendant that the four beasts represented four kings to arise out of the earth, but that the saints [NRSV; "holy ones"] of the Most High would receive the kingdom and possess it forever (Dan. 7:18).

Daniel had further quandaries about the fourth beast who made war on the saints until the Ancient of Days gave judgment and the holy ones possessed the kingdom. The attendant brought Daniel the answer that the fourth would be a kingdom different from others; it was to embrace the whole earth. It would have ten kings who would be followed by another who would throw down three kings. The king would be blasphemous, would persecute the saints, and would change times and seasons. But after a period a court would sit in judgment, his kingdom would be taken away, and the saints would possess the everlasting kingdom. The dominion of the other kingdoms would be taken away; this one would be completely destroyed. Kingship and everlasting dominion would be given to the saints of the Most High. Daniel was terrified, turned pale, but kept the matter in his mind. This scene influenced the Apocalypse where four creatures are described (cf. Rev. 4:7ff.).

It can hardly be doubted that the four beasts of this vision represent the same kingdoms as the various parts of the image seen by Nebuchadnezzar in chapter two. Jerome identified the fourth beast with

Rome. Porphyry, however, claimed that the leopard was Alexander the Great and that successors of Alexander were the fourth beast. He saw the ten kings as taking one to Antiochus Epiphanes whom he saw as the mouth speaking great things. Jerome saw this one to be the figure of 2 Thess. 2:8. Those today who interpret the fourth kingdom as Greece identify the "little horn" with Antiochus Epiphanes. Some who identify the fourth kingdom with Rome tend to interpret the "little horn" as a reference to a future Antichrist. E.J. Young insisted that the little horn of this chapter is not to be identified with the little horn of ch. 8. This one emerges from the fourth kingdom, that one from the third.

Yet again in the vision of ch. 7 the one like a son of man comes on the clouds of heaven *to* the Ancient of Days to receive a kingdom—which thing Jesus did at his ascension (Acts 1:9)—and not *from* the Ancient of Days to establish a kingdom as popular eschatology asserts that he will do at his second coming. There is no material here for outlining in advance how history is yet to go.

One of the major issues about this passage is that of whether the son of man in Daniel is the people of God or is the Messiah. Nowhere in Scripture do people receive such worship; hence, the description hardly fits the people of God. This passage is the ultimate source for the "Son of Man" concept in Messianic speculation. Jesus regarded himself as that Son of Man (Matt. 26:64), apparently quoting Dan. 7:13, 14.

The Vision of the Ram and the Male Goat, Ch. 8

A vision dated in the third year of Belshazzar is two years after the one narrated in chapter 7. Daniel sees himself in Susa by the river Ulai. A ram with two horns, one longer than the other, before which none could stand was pushing westward, southward, and northward. But a male goat from the west who advanced with such speed he appeared to move without touching the ground clashed with the ram, broke his horns, overcame him, and then magnified himself. But at the height of his power his horn was broken and four horns toward the four winds of heaven came in its place.

A little horn came out of the four and grew great and trampled some of the stars of the heaven. He trampled the continual burnt offering underfoot. A voice of a holy one stated that the vision was for 2,300 evenings and mornings, that is, for 1150 days (a period just exceeding three years), until the sanctuary was restored to its rightful state.

As Daniel tried to understand the vision, he heard one calling on Gabriel to help him. Daniel fell prostrate, went into a trance, but was touched by Gabriel. He was told the vision was for the end times. Gabriel (cf. Dan. 9:21; Luke 1:19, 26) explained that the kings of Media and Persia (Dan. 8:20) are the ram with two horns and that the male goat was the king of Greece (Dan. 8:21) from whom four kingdoms would arise. The horn between the eyes of the goat is its first king.

Gabriel, addressing Daniel as a mortal, speaks of a king arising at the end of the rule of the four kings who will destroy the people of the holy ones, rising even against the Prince of princes. However this king will be broken by power other than by human hands.

Daniel is told to seal up the vision for it is for many days from his time, but he was so overcome that he was sick for days before he could do the king's business. He was dismayed by the vision and did not understand it.

It seems obvious that the career of Alexander the Great (who died in Babylon in 323 B.C. at age 33) and the division of his kingdom among his four generals are described. It is usually thought that the little horn that arises is Antiochus Epiphanes (175-164 B.C.) whose career is surveyed in 1 Maccabees. Antiochus profaned the Jewish temple in 168 B.C. in an attempt to stamp out the Jewish religion. In the vision the temple would be restored after 2,300 evenings and mornings (Dan. 8:14) which would be 1,150 days or 3 1/2 years. The Jewish temple was actually desecrated in 168 B.C. and cleansed in 165 B.C. and sacrifice was restored. Jerome saw this figure as being Antiochus Epiphanes but thought him to be a type of the Antichrist.

The Vision of the Seventy Weeks, Ch. 9

Daniel's vision of the seventy weeks, dated in the first year of Darius, son of Ahasuerus, a Mede, is a development of Jeremiah's prophecy that the captivity must last seventy years (Jer. 25:11-13; 29:10ff.; cf. Zech. 1:12). Daniel's prayer in chapter 9 takes up far more space (16 verses) than the vision of seventy weeks (4 verses) but gets far less attention in modern speculation than the weeks. Confessing his own and his people's sinfulness (cf. Moses, Exod. 32:31-32; Paul, Rom. 9:1-3), Daniel with fasting and sackcloth and ashes acknowledges that God's threats stated in the Law of Moses have been accomplished in Israel's sufferings. He openly and unashamedly admits that he and his people have sinned. He prays that God may take his wrath from Jerusalem and make his face to shine upon the desolate sanctuary. No righteousness of the people can be offered, but Daniel appeals to God's great mercy and to God's concern for his own reputation (cf. the doctrine of "for the sake of his name" elaborated in Ezek. 20) since the city of Jerusalem and the people bear his name.

Gabriel again appeared to Daniel, this time at the time of the evening sacrifice. Gabriel states that there are to be seventy weeks to finish transgression and to bring in eternal righteousness. From the issuing of the decree to restore Jerusalem until the coming of an anointed prince is to be seven weeks. Then after sixty-two weeks the anointed one is to be cut off. The city will be destroyed. The prince will make a covenant, but for a half a week will cause sacrifice and offering to cease, and upon the wings of abomination will come the one who makes desolate (cf. Dan. 9:27; 11:31; 12:11; Matt. 24:15; Luke 21:20) until the decreed end is poured out upon the desolater.

Unlike the preceding vision of the ram and goat (Dan. 7), the seventy weeks are not interpreted to Daniel. Few biblical passages have been the subject of more speculation than has this one. Most systems of eschatology which calculate "times and seasons" depend in some way on these weeks. The passage is not interpreted or alluded to in any N.T. passage. While the Hebrew text (using only sevens [shebh`im]) does not specify the units of time used, if we assume that they are years (as the RSV and NRSV do), we would seem to be dealing with 490 years divided into three sections. The first has seven weeks or forty-nine years; the second has sixty-two weeks or 434 years; and the third has one week or seven years. But the starting and ending places of these periods remain completely uncertain.

Though the number of systems attempting to unravel Daniel's seventy weeks is legion and their complexities staggering, three may be taken as typical. First is that espoused by the historico-critical school which assumes that the sixty-nine weeks end in 171 B.C. when

Antiochus took the temple and desecrated it in 168 B.C. At this time Onias III, the faithful priest was cut off (cf. 1 Macc. 1:31, 32, 38; 3:45). The later defeat of Antiochus fulfills the prophecy. This system has to assume that the author of Daniel was mistaken, for no logical starting point (445, 586, 597, or 606 B.C.) takes one to 171 B.C. Furthermore, the author really sees another period following the Greek age before the Messianic kingdom. Hence, the vision must go beyond the Maccabean period.

Another system is that expounded in the notes of the Scofield Bible and by those of like mind who assume that the calculation starts at 445 B.C. (Nehemiah's return) and that rather than a year of 365 days the Jews used one of 360 days. By this juggling of the date the system comes out at A.D. 30, the time the system assigns to the rejection of Jesus by his countrymen. It is insisted, however, that at this point the prophetic clock ceased to run. The church-age (which the system considers to be unforeseen in prophecy) sets in. In this system when Jesus comes for his saints at the end of the church-age the seventieth week which includes the period the system calls "The Great Tribulation" will then take place.

Despite the popularity of the system among dispensational premillennialists, it has great difficulties. The Jews allowed for intercalation to keep their calendar in balance; hence, the case for the shorter year is not convincing. Furthermore, the seventy years of exile of Jeremiah which are the take off point of Daniel's vision (Dan. 9:1f.) are consecutive. The text of Daniel has no indication that his own sevens are not consecutive as the system assumes that they are not. Furthermore, already the alleged parenthesis between the sixty-ninth and the seventieth week has run four times longer than all the rest of the sevens put together. To say the least, the perspective of the system is out of joint.

A third system is the traditional one which begins the count with the rise of Cyrus and ends the first seven with Nehemiah in 445 B.C. The next sixty-two weeks (62 x 7) then brings one to Jesus, and the seventy weeks end at A.D. 70. The prince to come in this system is Titus. All in all, this seems the most satisfactory interpretation though even it is not without difficulties.

The King James Bible translates "anointed one" by "the Messiah the Prince" (9:25; *mashiach naghidh*) and "Messiah" (Dan. 9:26) identifying that figure with Jesus Christ, and the NIV capitalizes the two words "the Anointed One." Historically the Christian church has tended to interpret the passage Messianically. A literal rendering would be "an anointed prince" (v. 25) and "an anointed one" (v. 26).

The Kings of the North and South. Chs. 10-12

In the third year of Cyrus (535 B.C.), Daniel (who had now been in exile seventy years), after weeks of mourning, saw a vision while on the banks of the Tigris River. His companions fled out of fear so that Daniel alone saw a man whose face appeared as lightning and whose arms and legs were as burnished bronze and whose words sounded like the noise of a multitude. Daniel, having fallen with face on the ground, was raised up to be assured that the prince of Persia had withstood God, but that he would be succeeded by the prince of the Greeks. Michael (cf. Dan. 12:1; Jude 9; Rev. 12:7) came to Daniel's aid in this vision.

A sequence of three Persian kings is to be followed by a fourth richer than them all. He will stir up war with Greece whose mighty king will arise; but his kingdom will be divided into four parts, none of which are ruled by his posterity. The king of the south will be great. An alliance is made with the daughter of the queen of the south.

It seems clear that the section describes the rise of Alexander the Great and the division of his kingdom among his generals: Seleucus, Ptolemy, Lysimachus, and Antipater and his son Cassander. The Ptolemys (King of the south) and Seleucids (King of the north) struggled for domination of Palestine. The vision climaxes in description of the career of Antiochus Epiphanes (though of course he is not mentioned by name) and with his persecutions against the Jews. He profanes the temple (Dan. 11:31) and sets up the abomination that makes desolate—meaning a statue of Zeus (cf. 1 Macc. 1:54; Josephus, *Ant.* 10.11.7 [275-76]). Many Jews will apostatize and many will fall by the sword. The king will exalt himself above every god. Yet in the end he will be destroyed with none to help him. Daniel envisions the period to bring suffering such as has never been. But Daniel also envisions a resurrection of the dead both to everlasting life and to shame and everlasting contempt (Dan. 12:1-2).

Daniel is urged to seal up his book for the end times. When he inquired how long until the accomplishment of what he had seen was to be, he was told that there would be time, times, and half a time. From the time the burnt offering is taken away and the abomination of desolation is set up is 1290 days or 3.5 years. A blessing is pronounced on the one who waits. Daniel will die, but will stand in his place at the end.

Questions for Discussion

1. How does the second portion of Daniel differ from the first?

2. What is the distinctive feature of Daniel's dream?

3. What does the dream have in common with the narrative of Daniel 2?

4. What literary features of the book of Daniel are influential in later literature?

5. How does the book of Daniel influence later Messianic motifs?

6. What role does Gabriel play in the book of Daniel?

7. How is Daniel affected by his visions?

8. What are the significant ways of interpreting the seventy weeks of Daniel?

9. What outcome does Daniel see in the clash of the king of the north and the king of the south?

10. What role does the resurrection of the dead play in the O.T.?